Cities and Fiscal Choices

Duke Press Policy Studies

Cities and Fiscal Choices

A New Model of Urban Public Investment

Michael A. Pagano and Richard J. T. Moore

Duke University Press   Durham 1985

Library of Congress Cataloging-in-Publication Data
Pagano, Michael A.
Cities and fiscal choices.
(Duke Press policy studies)
Bibliography: p.
Includes index.
1. Municipal finance—United States. 2. Capital
investments—United States. 3. Infrastructure
(Economics)—United States—Finance. 4. Grants-in-aid—
United States. 5. Urban policy—United States.
I. Moore, Richard J. I. Title. III. Series.
HJ9145.P34 1985   336.02′73   85-16211
ISBN 0-8223-0653-0

This book is dedicated to
Deborah, Gina, and Andrea
and
Merced and Alexis Ramona

Contents

Tables and Figures

Tables

Figures

Preface

Much has been written of late regarding the "crisis of America's decaying infrastructure." Symptoms of malaise have been identified at all levels of government. Most of the extant literature either describes the condition vaguely, or proffers facile interpretations of the underlying causes. This volume is intended to fill part of the gap between these two treatments. In addition, this volume attempts to add to our understanding of decision making at the local level.

Drawing upon published and unpublished (field-based) data, four principal threads weave their way through our treatment. First, we argue that one cannot determine what government should do with regard to financing physical infrastructure unless one first understands the role that infrastructure plays in the economic development process. We examine the theoretical literature from developmental economics and public finance, and begin by placing the financing of infrastructure within the broader context of governmental responsibilities. Providing infrastructure, or public capital stock, is one of the major activities performed by government, but the financing of infrastructure for developmental activities is in dynamic tension with changes in redistributive policies across time, is contingent upon fiscal resources, and varies across governmental levels.

Focusing on infrastructural development at the municipal level in nine cities, the remaining three threads of this volume attempt to investigate this dynamic tension. First, we challenge the common argument that the reason for poorly maintained or insufficient construction of infrastructure can be explained in terms of local fiscal stress, and conclude that although fiscal stress is an important constraint on infrastructural development, it has been overplayed. Second, we challenge the common argument that the intergovernmental (federal) grant system is responsible for the current crisis. We conclude that although federal grants affect total outlays and, in some cases, project selection, they do not affect the commitment of local resources to capital investment. Finally, we develop a theory of local capital investment based upon incremental decision making. The failure to apply such a theory has led to an intergovernmental grant policy and a focus on fiscal scarcity that have been inappropriate in light of the need for infrastructure. Our review of the application of this argument to recent federal policies for local infrastructural development finds such policies wanting.

Many people have been instrumental in making this volume a reality. Both authors were senior policy analysts at CONSAD Research Corporation in Pittsburgh when CONSAD received a contract from the U.S. Department of Commerce to study public works investment in the United States (CONSAD 1980). Our responsibility was to collect field data from nine cities on the condition of and expenditure for urban infrastructure. Much of the data referred to in this volume were collected while we worked on this contract. We would like to thank Dr. Wilbur Steger, president of CONSAD, for use of this data base. We also appreciate the input of Richard Nathan (chapter 2), Patrick Larkey (chapter 3), Nancy Beer, the students of an urban policy seminar at Miami University (chapter 4), the students of a policy workshop on infrastructure at Princeton's Woodrow Wilson School, and anonymous referees for elaborate and useful critiques of the manuscript. The typing skills of Dorothy Pierson and Jean Roe are gratefully acknowledged, as well as their abilities to decipher our penmanship. Finally, we would like our families to know that without their constant encouragement, schedule reshufflings, and general support, this work would never have been completed.

Errors of omission and commission we perfunctorily assume are the fault of the other.

Michael A. Pagano, Miami University
Richard J. T. Moore, Princeton University

September 1984

Abbreviations

ACIR Advisory Commission on Intergovernmental Relations
AFDC Aid to Families with Dependent Children
ARFA Anti-Recessionary Fiscal Assistance
CBO Congressional Budget Office
CDBG Community Development Block Grant
CETA Comprehensive Employment and Training Act
EDA Economic Development Administration
EOC economic overhead capital
EPA Environmental Protection Agency
ETJ extraterritorial jurisdiction
FAUS Federal-Aid Urban System
GRS general revenue sharing
HUD Department of Housing and Urban Development
IRA Individual Retirement Account
IRB Industrial Revenue Bond
LPW Local Public Works Act, 1976 and 1977
MFOA Municipal Finance Officers Association
PSE Public Service Employment
RAN Revenue Anticipation Note
RFC Reconstruction Finance Corporation
SOC social overhead capital
UDAG Urban Development Action Grant
UMTA Urban Mass Transit Administration

1. *Public Capital Investment and Economic Development*

The Current Crisis

One of the traditional activities of urban and local governments—the construction, maintenance, and repair of infrastructure—has come under enormous scrutiny and criticism in recent times. As publicity about the problem of deteriorating infrastructure increases, commentators report that without adequate maintenance and public capital investment, cities and whole regions cannot expect to realize economic growth. One of the most noted authorities on the infrastructure avers, "One of the few advantages that old, larger cities possess in competing for economic activity is their inherited capital stock" (Peterson 1978, 49). The implication is that the capital stock of cities attracts economic activity.

The above statement—and much of the extant literature on the crisis of America's public infrastructure—implies, or explicitly argues, that investment in infrastructure is a necessary ingredient in firms' decisions to locate or expand at specific sites. To the extent that infrastructure is inadequate, the growth potential of any location becomes questionable. Cities are faced with a survival imperative that demands continued investments in existing and new public stock.

This book addresses the issue of infrastructure and the local determinants of the infrastructure problem. However, we propose to take two steps back from the immediate vicissitudes of falling bridges and crumbling concrete, and place the issue of public provision of infrastructure in a broader context. That is to say, as a means of understanding the infrastructure problem, we concern ourselves with the question of what cities *do* in contemporary America.

That sounds like a rather sweeping agenda for one short volume. Let us clarify our objectives a bit. This study focuses on cities and their performances of developmental functions. Much has been made of late about whose responsibility it is to do what in the American federal system. From politicians and their advisors we hear suggestions about revamping the federal system; from academics we hear of "proper functions" that cities realistically can be expected to perform. From all accounts we hear that cities (and perhaps the federal system as well) have been inadequately performing the basic function of providing appropriate public goods, among which infrastructure is counted.

If developmental functions are a major part of what cities do, then the issue of infrastructural investment, the apparent deterioration of existing public capital stock, the possibility of net disinvestment in public infrastructure, and the implications of deterioration all become important for several reasons. First, the provision of infrastructure plays several roles in the capital formation process and is therefore important. Second, the evidence of deterioration of waterways, transportation networks, sewer systems, etc., is alarming in and of itself and merits discussion. Finally, from an analytical perspective, an understanding of how and why urban governments have allocated resources for public infrastructure may tell us a great deal about broader (i.e., developmental and redistributional) policy choices that cities make.

Both the popular media and a plethora of studies in the past few years have assumed that neglect of public works investment or infrastructure means that cities have failed (and will continue to fail) to realize economic growth potential. A further assumption is that declines in public works investment are the consequence of the deleterious effects of limited financial capacity to expend. Thus, the principal foci of the literature have been the function and condition of infrastructure, the fiscal crisis of cities and its impact on public investment, and the changes and cutbacks in federal grants and their effects on local public investment. An intensive examination of these foci for all American cities would be impossible.[1] Therefore, as a means of understanding the issues, we restrict our scope to an analysis of three major infrastructural activities (street and bridge networks, water systems, and sewer systems) in nine geographically dispersed central cities.[2]

This volume examines the condition and the function of infrastructure (the remainder of chapter 1) and the separable impacts of fiscal stress (chapter 2) and federal grants (chapter 3) as predictors of infrastructural condition. However, we are somewhat discomforted by the "passivity of local government as actor" argument that is implied in these approaches. As we shall show, neither fiscal stress nor changes in federal aid proves to be an adequate explanation for investment or disinvestment decisions. Indeed, we argue, it is important to understand that cities make critical choices as to their own role(s). A city's willingness to expend, as shown in part by the patterns of expenditures, may tell us a great deal about the "how" and "why" of the current infrastructure crisis, and a great deal about the role of cities as providers of developmental or redistributional options. Chapter 4 offers an alternative framework for understanding public capital investment decisions. Finally, we conclude this volume by reexamining recent urban policy — particularly national urban policy — in light of how policy has responded to local perceptions of competing city needs based upon the alternative framework of chapter 4. The question addressed in this final chapter is: Has national urban policy been appropriate in responding to or in guiding the response of local government capital investment decisions?

Cities, Development Policies, and Capital Investments

Although infrastructure is often presumed to possess properties that attract economic activity, few studies on the determinants of industrial location and expansion present as unqualified a statement as that one. In fact, the industrial location literature suggests just the opposite: the activities of the public sector have a minimal effect on the decisions of firms to locate at one site compared with others. In spite of these findings, developmental policies are pursued vigorously by cities. In a recent volume, Paul Peterson (1981) suggests that cities pursue three qualitatively different policies. These "policy arenas" find their intellectual base in Lowi's (1964) policy typology. Peterson defines these three types of public policies in the following manner: "Developmental policies enhance the economic position of the city. Redistributive policies benefit low-income residents but at the same time negatively offset the local economy. Allocational policies are more or less neutral in their economic effects" (1981, 41). All city activities can be classified according to this typology. Because only developmental policies enhance the economic prospects of the city, Peterson claims that city governments' primary duties should be in developmental areas: "I find the primary interest of cities to be the maintenance and enhancement of their economic productivity. To their land area cities must attract productive labor and capital" (1981, 15). The other two types of policies do not have this enhancing effect; allocational policies have no impact on economic growth and redistributive policies have a negative economic effect. This definition of redistribution ("negative effects on local economies") represents a reduction of Peterson's original definition: "redistribution from the better off to the less well off segments of the community . . . [and] policies that have negative effects on local economies" (1981, 43). To illustrate this narrowing of definition, consider Peterson's discussion of air-pollution politics. He admits that it is hardly redistributive for all classes of people to enjoy the environmental benefits of the air-pollution programs, but he adds that "the adverse economic effects of strict air pollution control create problems for local policy makers similar to those raised by low-income housing programs and other obviously redistributive questions" (1981,

168). The standard has shifted for classifying a program as redistributive. The implication is that what is not developmental must be redistributive. More precisely, policies are really developmental or antidevelopmental, with a small grey area between the two that Peterson calls allocational. Allocational policies include the "traditional" areas of governmental involvement: justice, administration, law enforcement, and other "housekeeping" duties. Similarly, Musgrave (1959) suggests that allocational policies deal with providing social goods (nonrivaled and nonexcludable goods).

Although Peterson acknowledges that "most of what is discussed as urban politics is the politics of allocation" (1981, 150), he prefers to concentrate on the developmental and redistributive (antidevelopmental) policies of cities. Either policies enhance the economic position of a city or they don't. Peterson argues that redistributive policies necessarily increase marginal costs to the above-average taxpayer and firm, and developmental policies increase the benefits received. Indeed, we argue that this is the fundamental choice of cities in the budgetary process. Thus, a twofold typology that classifies activities according to whether or not they enhance activity can be constructed. The advantage of constructing a developmental/ antidevelopmental policies typology rests on the fact that it avoids the delusion that transfers (redistributions) are the real culprits in declining economies. Instead, it forces the question of distinguishing between policies designed to enhance economic growth and those without that immediate, specific objective.

Indeed, such a typology has been proposed previously. Niles Hansen proposed, as early as 1965, a typology that is surprisingly similar. Using a common concept in the economic development literature, "overhead capital," Hansen constructs a useful typology for understanding city policies. Overhead capital, or "social overhead capital," as Albert Hirschman calls the same cluster of activities, "is usually defined as comprising those basic services without which primary, secondary, and tertiary productive activities cannot function. In its wider sense, it includes all public services from law and order through education and public health to transportation, communication, power and water supply, as well as such agricultural overhead capital as irrigation and drainage systems" (Hirschman 1958, 83). Overhead capital, according to this scheme, comprises one basic set of economic activities; the other is "directly productive activities," or the actual production and distribution of industrial and agricultural goods.

Hansen attempts to sharpen the concept of overhead capital in order to identify and analyze the causes of municipal investment. He proposes to distinguish between those types of overhead capital that "are primarily oriented toward the support of directly productive activities or toward the movement of economic goods" (1965, 50), such as roads, power and water, communications facilities, sanitation services and sewerage, and those activities that are noneconomic in nature, such as fire and police protection, health and welfare, public housing, and education. The former category of activities he labels economic overhead capital (EOC), and the latter social overhead capital (SOC).[3] Stuart Holland, utilizing Hansen's typology, presents a view very similar to Peterson's concerning the impact of qualitatively distinct policies. He argues that SOC "is not essential for the efficient undertaking of directly productive activity, and that the provision of EOC alone is a necessary condition for it." He goes on to add that "while the provision of SOC alone does not necessarily result in the attraction of industry to an area, the location of directly productive activity utilizing available EOC will increase income and thus local taxation receipts from the firms concerned and employees, which can be utilized for the improvement of SOC" (1976, 216). In other words, cities' policies should be analyzed according to their impact on the economic activity of the community (Peterson 1981). In our discussion of the infrastructure, we adopt this framework.

In our treatment, EOC policies are those that promote economic activity; SOC policies are those that do not. One reason for the neglect of the nation's infrastructure is the failure to distinguish between EOC and SOC. Senator Daniel Patrick Moynihan voiced concern about this issue when he complained that "it continues to be the case that New York receives more 'soft' money than 'hard' [from the federal government]. The faster growing regions of the country get infrastructure, we get food stamps" (1979, 6). The implication of Moynihan's comments is that soft money is antidevelopmental and retards economic activity, while hard money is developmental and promotes economic growth.

The recent calls by Pat Choate (1981), Congressman William F. Clinger (R-Pa.) and Robert Edgar (R-Pa.), Peter Goldmark (Director of the Port Authority of New York and New Jersey), and recent congressional hearings (National Infrastructure Advisory Committee 1984) for the federal government to alter its budgetary practices to include a separate capital budget would aid in addressing this problem. A capital budget would be one way of not only monitoring and accounting for federal capital investments, but also keeping track of which regions or cities receive inadequate/disporportionate capital funds. Local governments generally maintain some sort of capital budgets. They know how much has been invested in any particular EOC (or SOC) category so that investment trends can be analyzed. However, we argue that local governments do not generally develop comprehensive capital budgets. If capital budgets are records of the fixed assets of cities, then they should include records of activities that clearly support or maintain that fixed investment. Capital budgets should have operating budget components that pertain directly to the maintenance expenditures of facilities: not street sweeping, but pothole repairs; not janitorial expenses for the water plant, but pipeline repair; and any other maintenance activities that either extend the useful design life of a facility, or allow the predicted useful life of the facility to be reached. For it is both kinds of activities that contribute to the utility and usability of EOC activities. Separating all EOC expenditures of both capital and operating natures from SOC outlays would surely help identify effects of policy shifts over time.

For now, the distinction between EOC and SOC provides a foundation upon which we can build. Instead of focusing on both policy types, we propose to follow Paul Peterson's and Holland's advice. Peterson claims that: "Cities, like all structural social systems, seek to improve their positions in all three of the systems of stratification—economic, social, and political—characteristic of industrial societies . . . [and] inasmuch as improved economic or market standing seems to be an objective of great importance to most cities, I shall concentrate on this interest" (1981, 22). Holland (1976) adds that the provision of EOC programs can be considered a necessary condition for improved economic or market standing. We propose, therefore, to focus the remainder of this book on EOC policies and their implications for the infrastructure debate.

The Role of Infrastructure in Development

We suggest that the public provision of infrastructure serves three important interrelated purposes. The first is as a foundation for economic growth. The second purpose is as an element of overall capital formation. The third is to reduce the costs of production for firms, thereby contributing to private capital formation.

The first purpose of infrastructural activities and public investment is to establish a foundation upon which directly productive activities can operate. Without the provision of adequate streets, water supply, and sewage treatment, it would be difficult indeed for directly productive activities to proceed, at least without tremendous cost to the producer. As a foundation for economic growth and for the introduction/expansion of directly productive activities, infrastructure can be provided in one of two ways. According to many developmental economists, government investment can direct or indicate the kind and quality of directly productive activity needed at a particular location. Such public outlays indicate points where private risks might be lessened. For example, Hirschman (1958) argues that according to backward- and forward-linkage industrial development analysis, the public sector should identify growth areas and provide appropriate goods and services in order to stimulate private investment. His approach requires an understanding of where sectoral bottlenecks develop so that government outlays can smooth the industrialization process and avoid contributing to more bottlenecks.

Many public finance and urban economic specialists, on the other hand, argue that public investments are a reaction to constantly changing levels of demand. As demand increases, the public sector must meet the new demand or face the possibility of losing firms and taxpayers to competing municipalities (Tiebout 1956). The public sector is thus viewed as an organization that reacts to constantly changing levels of demand.

Without engaging ourselves in the debate between these different perspectives on the timing of public investments (which is developed extensively in Chapter 4), it is instructive to note that they both recognize the vital importance of infrastructure to overall economic growth and development. Both argue that infrastructure is a foundation for economic activity or, as Holland argues, a "necessary condition" for the "efficient undertaking of directly productive activity" (1976, 216).

The second purpose for providing infrastructure restates and focuses the first. It suggests that the public sector's provision of infrastructure should be viewed as a vital and necessary aspect of capital formation. Infrastructure, or overhead capital, as Youngson argues, "seldom produces direct effects only, because the output of overhead capital is usually an input elsewhere in the economic system. . . . Usually, the opportunities created by overhead assets . . . are efficiently and fully utilized only as a result of the creation of further additional capital for setting up new productive activities or expanding old activities" (1967, 121). In other words, EOC must be understood in terms of its contribution to economic activity. Thus, creation or expansion of facilities must be realized before EOC can be considered as having had an impact on capital formation. From this perspective, although EOC activities are provided as inputs into the production process, such activities are considered vital to economic activity. Of course, much depends on the nature of the local economy in question. For example, developing societies emphasizing the expansion of industrial development have qualitatively different infrastructural needs than industrialized societies. Developing nations may require new port and highway facilities for industry, whereas industrialized nations may want to meet the needs of an ever-expanding service sector by providing better mass transit or communication services. In either context, public investment must adapt to the dynamic economic transformations of society in order to be an efficient agent in the capital formation process.

A third purpose for providing infrastructure is to expand the role of capital formation to include a dimension of who pays and who benefits. Firms that locate to minimize costs or maximize profits usually do not possess the capital to construct the necessary highway, water, sewer, and utilities systems required to engage in business. Goodrich (1960) argues that during the canal and railroad era in the first half of the nineteenth century, individuals had insufficient capital to undertake many necessary internal improvements. Therefore, much of the capital was raised by local, state, and national governments. Such socialized investment promoted westward expansion and economic activity (see, for example, Hartz 1968).

The costs of such basic infrastructure are usually borne by the taxpayers of the political jurisdiction within which the firm operates. The costs are socialized across the entire community to benefit the firm directly. Such "inputs," as Youngson (1967) calls them, are relatively costless to the firm. By employing individuals, the firm then contributes to the tax base of the community. In one sense, then, both residents (through an expanded tax base) and firms (through reduced costs) benefit, although the costs are disproportionately shouldered by the individual taxpayers.

Hence, the infrastructural or EOC activities of cities can be thought of as serving several interrelated roles. Traditionally discussed as a foundation for economic growth by developmentalists, EOC activities also contribute to capital formation and can stimulate individual firms or broader regional economic growth. On the other hand, inadequately provided EOC activities may have the opposite effect, and may retard economic activity. Much of the current discussion about the future of cities' capital stock indicates that this negative effect does occur. For example, U.S. Steel has claimed that it costs approximately $5 million per year in additional transportation costs because of a weight restriction on a poorly maintained bridge in the Pittsburgh area (Moore and Pagano 1982b). Had the bridge been maintained at appropriate levels the extra costs of doing business at that particular location would not occur. When the capital stock of cities does not perform at adequate levels, it may not have the developmental qualities that it was thought to possess. Thus, George Peterson's comment that the inherited capital stock of older cities gives them an advantage in competing for economic activity has a double thrust. Such a capital stock may serve not only as a determinant of industrial location, but also as a foundation for economic activity. George Peterson's concerns about maintenance practices and appropriate investment levels square with our understanding of the role of EOC: unless provided in adequate quantity and maintained at appropriate levels, infrastructure cannot necessarily be considered a developmental advantage for cities. It becomes developmental to the extent that it is functional in providing a base for economic growth and in reducing costs of directly productive activity. All of these roles, however, have at their root the theoretical capability of promoting economic activity; that is, they all serve developmental policy purposes.

The Growing Alarm: America in Ruins

It is not simply from the perspective of developmental economics that concern over the condition of America's capital stock has arisen. More popular attention has focused simply on the issue of physical decay. During the 1970s, particularly after 1974, there began to be a general concern about urban fiscal stress. In the past several years, there has been a barrage of literature focusing this concern on the issue of decaying urban America (*Newsweek* 1982). A mere perusal of the titles of some recent literature, from popular magazine articles to congressional reports, indicates that the era of pothole politics is upon us. Several examples will suffice: "Our Bridges are Falling Down" (*Parade*, 7 January 1979); "To Rebuild America: $2,500,000,000,000 Job" (*U.S. News and World Report* 1982); *Deteriorating Infrastructure in Urban and Rural Areas* (U.S. Congress, Joint Economic Committee 1979); *America in Ruins: Beyond the Public Works Pork Barrel* (Choate and Walter 1981); "Infrastructure: A Nationwide Need to Build and Repair" (*Business Week*, 26 October 1981); *The Future of America's Capital Plant* (George Peterson 1980–82). More recent publications include Hanson 1984; *National Journal* 1982; *Congressional Quarterly Weekly Report* 1982; National Infrastructure Advisory Committee 1984.

The rising level of public consciousness has been promoted by the realization that the real level of capital investment at all levels of government has been declining for most of the past fifteen years, and that, as a consequence, the net value of federal public works actually has declined constantly throughout the same period. Congressional recognition of the possibility of net disinvestment was evident as early as 1977 when Paul McCracken testified to the Senate Committee on the Budget: "Public construction was, in 1976, about 13 percent lower than in 1971, in an economy whose real output was 14 percent larger. There is, in short, needed work to be done, and public construction has been lagging. U.S. spending on public construction is phenomenally low. In real terms it has fallen very, very sharply over the past several years" (1977, 45). Congressional concern led to several major studies in the late 1970s. These were carried out under the auspices of a number of executive departments, including the Department of Housing and Urban Development (HUD), the Department of Commerce, and the Economic Development Administration (EDA). The concern, as one study suggests, is that "America's public facilities are wearing out faster than they are being replaced (Choate and Walter 1981, 1).

The consequences of this net disinvestment is not evidenced solely in the absence of high levels of investment in new construction, although that in itself is quite serious. But perhaps more important, net disinvestment is manifest in the deterioration of already existing public capital stock. At the national level, the degree of deterioration is difficult to estimate because there is no comprehensive national inventory of existing public infrastructure. The need for such an inventory is one of the rationales for calls for a

Table 1.1   U.S. infrastructure projection, 1983 to 2000 (billions of 1982 dollars).

Component	Needs	Revenues	Shortfall
Highways and Bridges	$ 720	$455	$265
Other Transportation	178	90	88
Water	96	55	41
Sewer	163	114	49
Total	$1157	$714	$443

Source: National Infrastructure Advisory Committee (1984, 5).

national capital budget. Instead, we have important, but crude, "guesstimates" based on the intensive research of several studies. One set of studies conducted by the National Infrastructure Advisory Committee provides us with a rough estimate of national capital needs compared to expected revenues for the remainder of the century. As can be seen in table 1.1, there is an estimated shortfall of more than $400 billion. According to another conservative estimate of maintenance, rehabilitation, replacement, and some minimal upgrading of capacity in existing structures in four major categories, the federal government has an investment backlog of needs of some $500 billion currently (George Peterson 1984). Still others put the estimate as high as $3 trillion over the next several years (*Congressional Quarterly Weekly Report* 1982). No matter how great the shortfall, it is clear that investment needs are much higher than current funding levels. More important, as decisions to make these investments are delayed, the investment costs of achieving even what is currently needed will increase, and of course any future maintenance needs will add to the already burgeoning inventory of need (Choate and Walter 1981, 40–44).

But net disinvestment on the national level is not the only problem. Equally important is state and local net disinvestment over the past fifteen years. "Deterioration of public facilities is the result of a dramatic cutback in capital spending by states and localities—both on new projects and on repair and maintenance of aging facilities" (Morgan Guaranty Trust, July 1982, 11). For example, it is estimated that the New York urban region would need to invest $8.6 billion (1980 dollars) each year throughout the 1980s to catch up to needs. This sum, estimated on the basis of capital investment programs and budgets of the various regional jurisdictions, amounts to more than three times current expenditure levels (Regional Plan Association 1982, 43–47). A recently completed study of New Jersey's infrastructural needs concluded that $15.1 billion would have to be spent between 1983 and 1987 on transportation, water supply, and wastewater disposal to meet the state's capital needs (Lake 1983). In testimony on the region's infrastructural needs, the executive director of the Port Authority of New York and New Jersey estimated that the collective capital needs of the seventeen-county New York–New Jersey region over the decade of the 1980s would be $40 billion. Specifically, he noted that "capital reinvestment in the major cities of northern New Jersey was virtually non-existent" (Goldmark 1982). Thus, not only the national government but also government at the subnational levels have not provided adequate funding for current and future capital needs.

Another reason for the rising level of public concern for the condition of public capital stock has been the occurrence of serious breakdowns and the increasing number of reports of the inefficient usage (and increased costs of repair) in specific major public facilities as a function of deferred maintenance. Information of this sort tends to be anecdotal rather than systematic, but it is alarming nevertheless. Examples include: the collapse of the Silver Bridge in West Virginia in 1968, leading to the creation of the National Bridge Inspection Program; the potential disaster of the weakened and near-collapse condition of New York City's Queensboro Bridge, which fortunately was discovered in time for "band-aid" repairs; the appearance of a dangerous crack in the Manhattan Bridge, which carries vehicles and subway trains between Manhattan and Brooklyn, as a result of acid corrosion of the steel due to long-neglected clogged drains in the runoff system of the bridge; a rupture in Jersey City's major aqueduct, which left the city and surrounding user communities without drinking water for six days in the summer of 1982; estimates that the city of Chicago had one million potholes at the end of the winter of 1981–82, and that New York paid $20 million in negligence claims due to unrepaired potholes in 1980; the bursting of an eighty-year-old earthen dam in Colorado that resulted in a wall of water flooding the town of Estes Park in the summer of 1982. Although these examples are more dramatic and more critical than the normal problems of poorly maintained facilities, they are not isolated. Neither is the problem of deteriorating facilities exclusively a problem of older northeastern cities, although age compounds the problem of maintenance.

A third reason for raised consciousness has been a visible change in the decision agenda in a number of cities to include what ordinarily is a very low political priority. Traditionally, only new public capital investment has offered political leaders opportunities for high visibility; maintenance and repair activities have received little attention or support. As one recent popular journal reported: "Have you ever seen a politician presiding over a ribbon cutting for an older sewer line that was repaired?" (*Newsweek*, 2 August 1982, 13). However, recent actions by a number of local political leaders and civic-action groups in cities such as Chicago, Pittsburgh, and New York have altered political perceptions of the problem. Mayors Byrne, Caliguiri, and Koch have all declared the urgency of devoting resources to repair. Maintenance has become an item in many local political agenda. In many of the cities, long-term neglect and deferral have raised political awareness of the importance of the issue. For example, Mayor Richard Caliguiri of Pittsburgh, after assuming the position of temporary mayor when Pete Flaherty resigned in the spring of 1977, bolstered his political support for the November elections by resurfacing almost 100 miles of the city's 900 miles of streets. He won the election without the endorsement of either political party by capitalizing on the fact that Flaherty's "austere" budget of the past six-year term had resulted in undermaintenance of the infrastructure. New York City, faced with large liability claims for vehicular damage due to neglected roadways, passed a pothole "prior notice" law that exempted the city from negligence claims in accidents unless the street defect had been reported fifteen days earlier. In response, a citizen's committee was formed—the Big Apple Pothole and Sidewalk Protection Corporation—to document and report street-repair needs.

Finally, the issue of public infrastructure needs and costs has found its way into national politics. Under the Carter administration, recognition came in the form of recommendations in the *National Urban Policy Report* of 1978 that cities be required to upgrade and renovate their deteriorating infrastructures as a condition for receipt of certain forms of federal aid (U.S. President 1978). The infrastructure problem was mentioned again in the President's Commission for a National Agenda for the Eighties report, *Urban America in The Eighties* (1980). More recently, there has been clamor in the face of both proposed and real budget cuts of the Reagan administration in areas of critical importance to maintenance activities. Cuts in Community Development Block Grants (CDBG) and concern over the future of general revenue sharing (GRS) funds are two examples of areas where maintenance and other operating revenues of local governments have been threatened.

The problem has been intensified by the impact of a plethora of monetary policy innovations at the national level that have led to increased competition among local borrowers and decreased incentives among lenders in the financial markets most utilized for resources for public capital investment (i.e., the tax-exempt municipal bond market). New programs such as All-Saver Certificates, individual tax credits, and rapid-depreciation allowances can trigger dramatic changes in the flow of investment funds. Even current programs of infrastructural investment and maintenance, particularly those in central cities already faced with critical problems of public capital stock and financial constraints, may be adversely affected in the years to come.

The Measurement of Physical Condition

Much of the recent alarm over the condition of the nation's public capital stock and estimates of needs presupposes a relationship between performance and condition. However, there exist few systematic methods of assessing infrastructural condition as related to capital needs. Recognizing the lack of general rules for assessing maintenance and replacement cycles, George Peterson (1976) developed five indicators of condition which, when taken together, provide some insight into the question of performance. Peterson's definition of *condition* does not include that dimension of performance that relates to the quantity or amount provided, but it does address the adequacy problem (for further analysis of condition and performance indicators, see CONSAD 1980; Huckins and Tolley 1981). Peterson's five indicators include: (1) direct observation; (2) maintenance and replacement cycles; (3) amount of capital investment needed to improve capital stock to adequate standards; (4) monetary losses due to public stock condition; (5) data on annual capital and maintenance expenditures.

The first of these, direct observation, is what most commentators and journalists note. Bridges are falling down! Expressway collapses! Water main bursts! Sewer and water systems leak underground! Observational techniques vary among infrastructural categories. The second indicator, maintenance and replacement cycles, depends on the explicit acknowledgment that capital stock wears out, as Huckins and Tolley (1981) suggest. To measure this, Peterson calls for collection of data on the miles of water pipe replaced each year, miles of street resurfaced, number of new mass-transit vehicles purchased and retired, tons of asphalt mix used for pothole filling, etc. Investment needs, the third indicator, provides estimates of how much must be spent to upgrade existing infrastructure, and how much will be required for new capital facilities. This indicator begs the question of whether these expenditures are really "needs" or merely "wish lists." The fourth indicator, private sector losses, is a measure of the direct impact of the damage that poor-quality capital stock can inflict on the users of the infrastructure. Factors such as waiting time due to public-transit breakdown, wear and tear on private automobiles from poor road and bridge conditions, street and basement flooding due to drainage back-ups, might be included. The final indicator is data on annual capital and maintenance expenditure. The financial arrangements, or the revenue sources available to local governments, should be examined in light of their appropriateness and responsiveness to a city's infrastructural needs. For example, what are the costs of maintaining particular structures and how have they changed over time? These five indicators, when taken together, could present a partly accurate picture of the public capital stock's condition, but there is a serious problem of how to collect data on these dimensions. Indeed, one of the most profound data problems in urban policy is the paucity of any good-quality information on direct expenditures for the infrastructure, on investment needs and replacement cycles, and on most every other aspect of infrastructure research.

But if infrastructure performance is to be understood and evaluated in the broader context of revenue constraints, federal program impacts, and competing needs, then accurate, comprehensive data are essential. Let's examine the data requirements. First, for direct observation to be valid, more data are required than newspaper stories on spectacular breakdowns provide. Direct observation should be an ongoing, continuous documentation effort on the part of those who know what to look for, e.g., civil engineers. Compiling data from preventive maintenance programs might be one way of standardizing the data. Unfortunately, urban data on preventive maintenance practices are not uniform, most likely because no uniform standards exist. Furthermore, because observation is not a reporting requirement for higher levels of government or for bond-rating agencies, data have not been collected in any standardized format at the state or federal level. Neither do such data appear in bond prospectuses published to generate the needed funds for particular capital projects.[4]

In the present study an attempt was made first to evaluate the condition of four categories of infrastructure in the nine cities from the perspective of "direct observation." The condition rating provided in table 1.2 should not be thought of as an absolute judgment. The rating for each functional area was based on the evaluation of various documents, information, and interviews in each city. It is our belief that the ratings are at least comparative in that a *fair* rating for one city is similar to a *fair* rating for another. Absolute and generally recognized measures are lacking, and formulas to determine a quantitative condition assessment do not exist. Nevertheless we hope that our careful use and examination of city information provide generally accurate estimated condition ratings.

Several comments on the condition of infrastructure, as determined through direct observation in our sample cities, are noteworthy. First, the condition of infrastructure for the two cities that are in good fiscal condition (see chapter 2), Dallas and Des Moines, ranks in the *fair–good* or better range for all four functional categories. Those cities that we identify (again in chapter 2) as fiscally stressed generally, especially Baltimore, Hartford, Newark, and St. Louis, appear to have poorly maintained capital stock. However, there are clear exceptions. Note that the water systems for all cities are rated at least *fair*, and that the sewer systems of most cities are in fair condition or better. We will argue in subsequent chapters that these condition ratings and their relationship to fiscal stress, functional category, and method of financing are important considerations. Also relevant in table 1.2 is the rather mixed picture of the condition of street and bridge systems, irrespective of the fiscal conditions of the city. Again, in subsequent chapters, we argue that something more than simple fiscal stress is needed to explain the relatively poor performance in these categories.

The second indicator of infrastructure condition—maintenance and

Table 1.2   Direct observation of condition for each functional area by city.

	Water System	Sewer System	Streets	Bridges
Poor and Deteriorating Rapidly				N,P
Poor		N (collection)		
Poor–Fair, but worsening			NO, H	H
Poor–Fair		N (treatment) SL	B, N, P, SL	B, NO, SL
Poor–Fair, but improving				
Fair, but worsening			S	
Fair	N (City) SL	P (collection)		S
Fair, but improving				
Fair–Good	B, NO, S N (regional)	B, S (collection)	D	
Good	D, H, P	D, H, DM, NO S (treatment)	DM	D
Good–Very Good		P (treatment)		
Very Good	DM			DM

Note: B = Baltimore; D = Dallas; DM = Des Moines; H = Hartford; NO = New Orleans; N = Newark; P = Pittsburgh; SL = St. Louis; and S = Seattle.
Source: CONSAD (1980, II.13).

replacement cycles for infrastructural activities—is usually not even reported at the local government level and is certainly not aggregated by state or required by higher level governments. The primary problem is that not enough is known about appropriate replacement cycles nor about the rate at which facilities wear out. A policy implication could easily be that cities should replace facilities after they wear out. How long that might be is anybody's guess. Standards either do not exist, or fail to dictate policy even when there is some modicum of agreement. Peterson (1976, 63) suggests that streets should be repaved on a ten- to twenty-five-year basis. However, that may be an inadequate standard upon which to develop a capital replacement program. One report, based on a compilation of information from engineering sources, suggests that age, paving materials, usage, weather conditions, soil characteristics, and maintenance practices affect the condition of streets and, hence, appropriate replacement cycles (CONSAD 1980, vol. IV). Although common sense might suggest that a street repaved every year—one-year replacement cycle—would be in excellent condition, it can hardly be concluded that cities should undertake such programs. Realistic recommendations for replacement cycles, based on scientific criteria and algorithms that take into account the variables mentioned above, have not reached a level of acceptable accuracy. Although data on replacement cycles should be collected for comparisons among cities, such data cannot be viewed as a standard measure of performance for all cities' infrastructures. Furthermore, for the most part, replacement cycles are not published, and must be reconstructed from city documents.

For the nine cities in our study, an attempt was made to establish street resurfacing cycles where data were available (table 1.3). Although the data are incomplete, what is clear is that there are wide differences among cities, and even in given cities over time. In part, this is because even the shortening of replacement cycles has been more a function of addressing a backlog of maintenance needs than an indicator of longer-term trends or of adequate maintenance programs. New Orleans, for example, paved nineteen miles of streets in 1977, which would indicate a cycle of eighty-four years; however, based on the average for earlier years, four to five miles per year, the cycles are closer to three hundred years!

A third indicator of infrastructure condition, public investment needs of cities as described by city officials, often amount to nothing more than "wish lists." Although some determination of "needs" is often incorporated into capital improvement plans, the idealized nature of such wish lists is clear. Assuming no monetary constraints, no labor shortages, no lack of expertise, and assuming that the facility will be used, how much capital is required to upgrade the infrastructure to appropriate levels? The real problem is how to define *appropriate levels*. In another context, O'Day and Neumann make the point succinctly in addressing national infrastructure needs:

Unfortunately, the approach taken to defining needs in many studies has been, and continues to be, very narrow and of limited usefulness in guiding resource allocation decisions at any level of government. In a recent speech focusing on the desirability of a national capital budget, Senator Tsongas from Massachusetts noted that Congress has no capability at all in dealing with needs estimates ranging from hundreds of billions to tens of trillions of dollars for the highway system. When confronted with such ranges, the needs estimates become almost irrelevant (1983, 2.1).

The fourth indicator of condition relies on probably the most difficult data to collect: the costs to the private sector due to the inadequate condition of the infrastructure. No systematic effort to estimate such monetary losses has been undertaken even by local governments.

Table 1.3   Street resurfacing cycles in nine cities.

City	Miles Resurfaced (year)	Resurfacing or Replacement Cycle
Baltimore	25 (1978)	50 years
Dallas	334 (1976–77)	24 years
Des Moines	22 (1977–78) (est.)	27 years (est.)
Hartford	<4 (1977–79)	50–100 years
New Orleans	19 (1977)	84 years·
	405 (1970–76)	320 years
Newark	13 (1976–78)	30 years
Pittsburgh	100 (1977)	9 years
	20 (1970–76)	46 years
St. Louis	NA	—
Seattle	86 (1976) (est.)	<20 years (est.)

Source: Field data.

The last indicator, expenditures, is probably the one best understood by urban policy analysts and public finance experts, and also the one that is presumed by many to be readily available and comparative across cities. Unfortunately this is true only at a crude level. Annual maintenance and capital expenditures represent the city's willingness and capacity to invest in and maintain the infrastructure. However, city expenditure publications by the U.S. Bureau of the Census have no *maintenance* item. Maintenance is part of the city's operating expenditures and is thus hidden under total outlays for a particular function, e.g., sewerage, highway transportation, water terminals. The total operating outlay figures include administrative, secretarial, clerical, janitorial, and minor equipment expenditures (non-capital), and also outlays for the workers who actually perform the maintenance activity, and materials and equipment for the activity (unless they are of sufficient monetary magnitude to be included under capital outlays). The separation of maintenance from other nonmaintenance operating expenditures is no mean task. Many cities do not disaggregate operating outlays in their budgets or annual financial reports. Such disaggregation has to be reconstructed from other documents.

But even if cities do separate maintenance expenditures as a specified subcategory in their budgets, budgets cannot be relied on as statements of actual outlays. The budget is a statement of intent, no more. For example, one major city in our study budgeted over $500,000 for street maintenance because it expected that amount from the state, based on a program that allocated gasoline tax revenues to cities. During the year, most of this revenue was allocated to other highway categories and departments, and actual street maintenance outlays were only $100,000. In this study, we attempted to collect only data on actual expenditures.

There is also a need for an analysis of public capital investment trends in light of financial constraints and changing sources of revenue. Some cities can no longer borrow funds for capital programs because of the high costs of borrowing; some that receive federal aid must undertake certain projects to be in compliance with federal regulations. Tracing revenue sources and the impact of certain types of revenue on the capital stock of cities would provide insight into the question of how much infrastructure is constructed and in what quantity and quality. Unfortunately, published documents do not include revenue sources for specific capital outlays. Public capital investment outlays are published, often by functional category, e.g., public buildings, water system, but revenue sources are never specified for those functions.

In sum, most of the data that might be useful in assessing the condition and performance of cities' infrastructure are not available in published form or are, at best, difficult to get. Records in some cities are in usable (although unpublished) form and little work is necessary to compile requisite data on infrastructural performance. Other cities' records require weeks and weeks of hunting and digging to dredge up even the most insignificant pieces of data, with the result in a few cases of unusable or incomplete data. Furthermore, time-series data are clearly superior to cross-section data. If an analyst were to evaluate outlays for New York City in 1981 alone, he might be inclined to report that fiscal condition, revenue, and spending were fine. But in the context of a fifteen- or twenty-year period, a different pattern emerges. Therefore, data need to be collected over time to measure performance in a longer-term perspective than just one, two, or even five years. These data, especially those that are not even published by the city, are often buried deep in the bowels of the city's files and are quite difficult to retrieve. Because of these data limitations, analysis must be confined to a small sample of the universe of cities. Hence, we use a case-study approach to analyze the performance of the infrastructure.

Data Collection

Due to time and monetary constraints, nine geographically dispersed central cities with varying degrees of fiscal stress were selected for in-depth study (for a further description of the selection process, see CONSAD 1980, vol. II). Although we make no claim that the sample of cities selected here is random, we believe they do represent reasonable variations in terms of a number of the criteria important for this study: relative fiscal stress, city age and implicit age of the capital stock, weather and other conditions that affect the infrastructure and its maintenance, city size, and city functional responsibility. A study team of approximately four analysts, one of whom was a civil engineer, visited each city for an average of sixteen person-days per city. The duration of the visits was a function of the difficulty in tracking and recording the data. For example, most cities knew how much each department was supposed to spend (budget) and how much each department spent (annual financial reports), but few cities had any readily available documents that detailed either actual capital expenditures by revenue source, or outlays for maintenance. Site visits were undertaken between 2 January and 16 February 1979. The cities were Baltimore, Dallas, Des Moines, Hartford, Newark, New Orleans, Pittsburgh, St. Louis, and Seattle.[5] The results of our analysis of these cities, we believe, will be applicable to many cities across the United States.

Because of the difficulty in retrieving the data, we focused our data collection efforts on (1) actual maintenance and capital expenditures and revenue sources for the 1957 to 1977 period, (2) records and other information that might indicate the physical condition of the infrastructure (i.e., direct observation), and to a lesser degree on (3) replacement cycles, to the extent available. Data were not collected systematically on investment needs, although direct observation often indicated what was needed, nor on private-sector losses, an almost impossible datum.

Following Holland (1976), Hirschman (1958), and Hansen (1965), infrastructure of EOC categories were defined, using Bureau of the Census categories: *highways, airports, water, sewerage, gas, electricity, urban renewal, transit, sanitation, parking facilities,* and *water transport* (or their equivalents). Instead of collecting data on all categories—a virtually impossible task—three categories or functional areas were selected: *water systems, sewer systems* (or *sewerage*), and *streets and bridges* (*highways*). These categories represent over 50 percent of total expenditures of all U.S. cities on infrastructure between 1974 and 1979. They also represent over 45 percent of all capital outlays for U.S. cities for the same time period. Over 100 city officials, or approximately 11 per city, were interviewed or in some way aided the data collection. After the site visits were completed, the data were scrutinized and appropriate city officials were contacted to discuss any problems. Site-visit reports, based on the information collected at each city, were sent back to an average of 5 officials in each city for their comments.

Summary

The past few years have witnessed growing evidence of the deteriorating quality of public capital stock at all levels of government. At the same time, there is clear evidence of growing disinvestment in the nation's infrastructure as well as undermaintenance of much of the existing infrastructure.

How can we account for the current physical condition of and investment trends in infrastructure?

In this chapter, we have argued that there is a need to step back from the vague outcries of the alarmist popular literature and, at the same time, from the descriptive approaches of some of the more serious attempts to document the condition of the nation's public capital stock. One cannot determine what government should do with regard to financing physical infrastructure unless one first understands the role that infrastructure plays in the economic development process. In this chapter we have examined the theoretical literature from developmental economics and public finance, and we have begun by placing the financing of infrastructure in the broader context of governmental responsibilities. As we have noted, providing infrastructure, or economic overhead capital (EOC), is one of the major activities performed by government, but the financing of infrastructure for developmental activities is in dynamic tension with redistributive policies of governments. Decisions as to the proper balance between developmental and redistributive policies change across time, are contingent upon fiscal resources, and may vary across governmental levels. In addition, we note that to suggest that infrastructure is in poor condition misses much of the point. Not all types of public capital stock, not all levels of government, and not even all cities are experiencing the impact of declining infrastructure. In part, we argue, it is because the playing out of this dynamic tension takes on different forms.

Focusing on infrastructural development and finance in our nine cities, the remaining three threads of this volume attempt to explore this dynamic tension. First, we challenge the common argument that the reason for poorly maintained or insufficient construction of infrastructure can be explained in terms of local fiscal stress, and conclude that although fiscal stress is an important constraint on infrastructural development, it has been overplayed (chapter 2). Second, we challenge the common argument that the intergovernmental (federal) grant system is responsible for the current crisis. We conclude that although federal grants affect total outlays and, in some cases, project selection, they do not affect the commitment of local resources to capital investment. Further, we develop a theory of local capital investment based upon incremental decision making and local willingness to invest (chapter 3). We then extend the theory to include trade-offs between EOC and SOC policies and place the infrastructure and developmental focus of the preceding chapters in the context of current city perceptions of economic growth (chapter 4). Finally, we argue that the failure to apply such a theory has led to an intergovernmental grant policy and a focus on fiscal scarcity that have been inappropriate in light of the need for infrastructure (chapter 5). We conclude by examining the application of this argument to recent federal policies for local infrastructural development, and we find such policies wanting.

2. Fiscal Stress and the Financing of

Urban Infrastructure

The quality of a city's infrastructure, the level at which it is maintained, the trade-off between providing infrastructure and/or social services, and the potential for improving any of these are all ultimately affected by one factor: the relative scarcity of available resources. A principal focus of many studies on the infrastructure is the problem of low fiscal capacity in various governmental jurisdictions. As George Peterson noted: "If significant underinvestment has occurred, it in turn implies some type of failure in the infrastructure financing system" (Peterson 1983, 2). A city's inability to generate revenues will adversely affect the condition of existing urban infrastructure, its maintenance, and capital outlays. Thus, fiscally stressed cities are unlikely to be able to perform their developmental functions adequately. This chapter will explore the relationship between fiscal stress and infrastructural expenditures, and the degree to which cities alter expenditure decisions because of fiscal stress.

As the previous chapter suggests, much has been made of late of the federal government's role in infrastructural finance and the "national problem" of rebuilding America's infrastructure. Yet most public investment in infrastructure occurs at the subnational level; states and local governments are the principal investors in public capital in the United States. Much of what we associate with the construction and upgrading of facilities is reflected in cities' capital budgets; maintenance activities appear as items in operating budgets or current accounts. Expenditures can be financed either by tax or nontax revenues, or by incurring debt. Even when debt issuance is the instrument of finance, capital financing and maintenance financing are two sides of the same coin: debt service is financed through current account revenues; the attractiveness of the purchase of debt is affected by the quality of existing revenue-generating capabilities; and crises in the bond market are usually felt in the entire budgetary process (Bradbury 1979). Thus, an examination of fiscal stress is an important beginning point.

The Issue of Growing Scarcity

Fiscal stress in American cities did not spring up overnight, nor did it begin with the New York City near-default in 1975. The allocation of scarce resources has always been a primary concern for every government, and city governments are no exception. Since the defaults of the Great Depression, however, cities rarely have faced the possibility of simply being unable to raise sufficient revenues—until, that is, the mid-1970s. This solvency was primarily because incomes and property values (the taxation of which provides major sources of revenue for cities) increased in the postwar period, as did state and federal aid programs that helped to ensure a revenue base for increasing the service delivery packages cities offered.

The expansion of service delivery programs was inspired by the availability of funds, whatever the source. Federal largesse in the 1960s often encouraged localities to spend out of proportion to their own local revenue-raising capacities. As Lineberry and Masotti note:

> The massive Federalization of urban programs . . . meant that cities established supermetropolitan ties which reduced the pressures for metropolitan solutions. . . . Model cities, sewer construction, library aid, law enforcement assistance monies, poverty funds, and . . . revenue sharing—marked a new dependence of the city on a rich benefactor. . . . As cities got more resources from the Federal government, they undertook more social services policies. Problems arose, however, when the pie threatened to stop growing (1976, 10–11).

One might add that the federal largesse affected not only the expansion of social service activities, but also involvement in infrastructural activities. However, the federal government was not the only extralocal actor involved in expanding the role of cities; states aided the expansion.

Extralocal aid programs stepped in to fill the void created by a fiscal squeeze in local own-source funding. The fiscal Catch-22 of local own-source receipts is that in order to increase revenue, taxes (principally property taxes) must be increased, which in turn invites residential abandonment of central cities. The 1970s witnessed a modest shift in the revenue structure of localities to more elastic forms, (such as sales and income taxes), and away from the overwhelming reliance on property taxes. In 1960, property taxes represented 70 percent of total locally generated receipts; by 1980 the proportion had dropped below 60 percent. However, the property tax burden in 1980 in per capita terms was more than four times the burden of 1960. Although the property tax is less significant for large cities than for local governments generally, it remains the dominant tax form. In addition, the attempted diversification can also have adverse consequences; local governments' ability to service existing debt and current operating expenses is more vulnerable to economic slowdowns when larger proportions of tax receipts are tied to elastic tax forms.

In the face of this own-source fiscal squeeze, the growth of federal aid to local governments (in the form of grants-in-aid) over the past twenty-five years has been nothing short of startling. According to census data reported in *Government Finances* (U.S. Department of Commerce), direct federal grants-in-aid to localities increased almost sixfold between 1957 and 1967, and eightfold between 1967 and 1977. The magnitude of the increase in the federal role is more easily comprehended when one compares the growth in federal funding to the growth of locally generated funds. Table 2.1 provides evidence of the trends in extralocal aid to all local governments over time. While all forms of extralocal aid increased substantially over the period, the dramatic growth of federal aid to localities is worth emphasizing in particular. In 1957, direct federal grants were equal to only 2 percent of own-source receipts for all localities; by 1967, such grants had increased to 5 percent; and by 1977, federal grants had increased to 16 percent and total extralocal (non-internally generated) aid equalled 75 percent of own-source receipts. By 1982, even with substantial cutbacks in federal programs, the equivalent percentages had declined to only 10.6 and 58.8, respectively.

While local revenues became increasingly scarce, the growing participation of the federal government allowed expenditures to continue to climb (Yin 1979). By the late 1970s, however, the rate of growth of federal grants-in-aid had slowed. This slowdown is even more dramatic given the rate of inflation for the period. Gramlich (1978) suggests that for all localities General Revenue Sharing (GRS) led to a budgetary surplus in the period after 1973; however, for urban governments the surplus was short-lived because the rate of growth of federal aid failed to keep pace with expenditures. By 1976, the surplus for urban governments had disappeared. It was at this point that the issue of fiscal stress and scarce resources at the local level became an issue on the national agenda.

Defining and Measuring Fiscal Stress

In the most basic sense, fiscal stress refers to the inability of a government to balance its budget. In this sense, it is a budgetary concept and can be measured by examining a variety of budget characteristics. In a broader sense, fiscal stress is a structural phenomenon, reflecting shifts in the social and economic conditions of the city.

Some activities, especially revenue raising and expenditure cutting, lie more readily within the purview of local decision making than others, but the costs of these activities may well be different for different jurisdictions. Bradbury notes that "any city can avoid immediate financial trouble by keeping its tax rate high enough or its locally controlled expenditures low

Table 2.1   Outside aid to local governments, 1957–1977
(millions of current dollars).

Year	Federal[1]	Other	State and Federal Aid to Local Governments	
			Amount	As Percentage of Local General Revenue from Own Sources
1957	346	7,209	7,554	43.2
1958	368[2]	NA	NA	—
1959	543[3]	NA	NA	—
1960	593	NA	NA	—
1961	719	10,185	10,904	43.6
1962	750	10,929	11,678	43.8
1963	890	11,799	12,680	44.5
1964	956	12,873	13,829	45.7
1965	1,155	14,077	15,232	46.6
1966	1,378	16,391	17,768	50.2
1967	1,889	18,507	20,395	53.2
1968	1,954	20,342	22,295	54.5
1969	2,245	23,837	26,082	56.9
1970	2,605	26,920	29,525	57.5
1971	3,391	31,082	34,473	60.0
1972	4,462	34,555	39,018	60.5
1973	7,903	39,963	47,866	67.9
1974	10,199	44,553	54,752	71.3
1975	10,906	51,068	61,974	73.5
1976	13,576	56,169	69,746	74.8
1977	16,637	60,311	76,948	75.4

1. Federal grants-in-aid to localities includes grants-in-aid to the District of Columbia.
2. Excludes Alaska and Hawaii.
3. Excludes Hawaii.
Source: U.S. Department of Commerce, Bureau of the Census, *Government Finances*, by year.

enough. But because of the external "structural" factors, it may be considerably more difficult for some cities to achieve a balance than others" (1979, 6). Although we are somewhat less sanguine than Bradbury about the possibility that "any city can" in any but the most theoretical terms, the thrust of the above statement is correct. However, Bradbury's last point is not negligible; many budget-balancing constraints are external (i.e., dependent upon national economic conditions) and structural, and thus are not subject to local control. Because of this, we should examine measures of revenue-raising capacity, relative burdens, and changes in socioeconomic conditions in dynamic terms, and not simply in terms of static decisions that involve balancing the budget in any given year.

Some scholars suggest that fiscal stress is affected by the degree of intergovernmental aid that a given jurisdiction receives. One argument is that the enticement of matching programs inspires local governments to spend more than they otherwise would have (Fainstein and Fainstein 1976). On the other hand, if increased intergovernmental aid results from the design of grants that incorporate "needs" into their formulas, more inter-governmental aid must be seen as a result of fiscal stress, and not the other way around.

The literature provides no clear and agreed-upon criteria for identifying fiscal stress. This has not been for lack of trying. One author identifies seventy-seven different measures that have been utilized in recent research efforts (Bradbury 1979). Among the approaches that have been proffered are those suggesting that fiscal crisis and stress are the result of: central-city flight and intrametropolitan disparities (Fuchs 1962; Thompson 1965); demands on specific "declining cities" to provide services or to raise wages at a time when revenue bases have shrunk (Meyer and Quigley 1977); debt-service requirements due to excessive borrowing in the past (Peterson 1976); poor leadership qualities, mismanagement, or improper actions by city officials (Clark and Ferguson 1983; Gerard 1976); different func-tional responsibilities of cities (Dye and Garcia 1978; Norton 1979); actions or inactions by the federal government that affect local expenditures (Fainstein and Fainstein 1976); regional imbalances and biases in the distribution and content of federal aid programs (Perry and Watkins 1977; Holland 1976; Sawers and Tabb 1984); and urban age, anachronistic cities, and the historical development of capitalism in the United States (Perry and Watkins 1977; Mollenkopf 1983). Each perspective—implicitly or explicitly—offers the reader a unique list of recommended policy options.

One of the difficulties in using any of these concepts of fiscal stress is that, with few exceptions, they tend to gloss over the specific conditions of individual cities, preferring instead to pursue macro-level comparisons.[1] Furthermore, studies rarely have attempted to gain a longitudinal perspec-tive on city fiscal performance, and have focused instead on describing the current crisis.

Each of these approaches offers some validity, and each implies a differ-ent set of analytic measures. Measures of budget distress might include such variables as surpluses (or deficits) in the operating budget (Gramlich 1978); the availability of liquid assets relative to existing claims on those assets (Touche Ross 1979); the relative magnitude and the burden of outstanding debt (Bahl, Jump, and Schroeder 1978; Aronson and King 1978; Clark and Fuchs 1977); comparative functional responsibilities and expenditures (Dye and Garcia 1978); revenue reliance and diversity (MacManus 1978); tax burden, tax rate, and tax effort (Advisory Commission on Intergovernmental Relations [ACIR] 1971; MacManus 1978); and the degree of reliance on intergovernmental aid (Ott et al. 1975). Each of these measures, in turn, can be manipulated in a variety of ways.

Different sets of measures are suggested by a focus on a locality's changing socioeconomic environment. For example, the costs of similar services vary across jurisdictions because of different input and production costs. Thus, expenditure requirements may differ, although these may be very difficult to measure due to overlapping jurisdictions and lack of effective controls. Some authors have offered indexes of the relative tax and service delivery burdens borne by central-city and surrounding jurisdictions as devices for capturing changing intrametropolitan conditions (Nathan and Adams 1976; Nathan and Fosset 1979). Other measures that attempt to capture an image of the changing socioeconomic circumstances under which a jurisdiction may be able to alter either its revenue or expenditure patterns might include such variables as population characteristics and change, income, incidence of poverty, employment characteristics and change, housing starts, age of housing, and so on.

Measures Used for this Study

The choice of variables in any research endeavor is guided in part by the purposes of the research. We are concerned with the relationship of fiscal condition and the two principal functions of city government: providing and maintaining infrastructure, and providing certain social services. This focus has led to our identification and examination of several indicators of fiscal condition and stress.

To aid us in examining budgetary stress and constraints on the fiscal capacity of a city, several measures are included in this analysis. The most important of these is the property tax rate, measured in terms of the effective rather than the nominal rate. The effective property tax rate is the ratio of the total tax bill to the fair market value of the property. We use the mill rate on fair market value as our property tax measure. It is important to note that the nominal rate can be very misleading as a comparative measure. As the U.S. Bureau of the Census notes: "One cannot use the nominal property tax rate because the wide variation in assessment ratios across communities implies that the actual rate at which a community taxes property is not likely to bear a systematic relationship to the nominal rates. . . . Effective rates usually lie substantially below nominal rates because market values which condition effective rates usually are substantially above assessed value" (cited in MacManus 1978, 10).

Property taxes comprise the largest single contribution to local governments' own-source receipts. Because most central cities that experience outmigration cannot counter the resulting revenue declines with equivalent service curtailments, property tax increases often become the "quick fix" solution to the problem. But the capacity to increase property tax rates depends on the magnitude of the existing tax burden, on legal restrictions on the tax rate, and also on the political acceptability of a tax increase. Both the property tax revolt and the political inability to raise property taxes in many cities suggest that the property tax cannot necessarily be considered as a safety valve to offset revenue shortfalls, even when the existing tax burden is relatively low.

The dimension of the political acceptability of a tax increase parallels to some extent the willingness of local officials to expend for a given package of activities (chapter 1). We tap the dimension here with a measure of tax burden, or as MacManus (1978, 10–11) notes, a "relative comparison of the 'bite' of taxes collected locally in relation to the income of the residents of that city." Our measure is calculated as a ratio between own-source revenues and income, each measured in per capita terms (tax burden = income per capita/own-source revenue per capita). Data for 1970 and 1975 are presented in table 2.2.

Several comments on the data presented in table 2.2 are warranted. First, the higher the ratio, the greater the bite of taxes, that is, the greater the tax burden. For both years shown, two cities (Newark and Hartford) experienced tax burdens significantly higher than the other seven cities. In 1970, that difference was as much as three times (for example, compare the burdens of Dallas, Des Moines and Seattle). Although the relative difference was lower in 1975, it remained significant. It is also worth noting that Newark and Hartford had the highest burdens of tax in another sense: the amount of revenue generated in per capita terms was dramatically higher than in other cities. This fiscal burden was also evident in a number of socioeconomic indicators.

In many ways, revenue growth potential is a function of property taxes, and the capacity to increase property tax rates is, in part, dependent on the size of the existing property tax burden, as well as on the relative reliance on property taxes as a source of own-source receipts. However, property tax increases are dependent not only on the existing tax burden and on legal restrictions on the tax rate, but also on the political acceptance of a tax increase. For example, New Orleans's residents are unwilling to raise their property tax rate, even though it is among the lowest in the nation. One chief administrative officer told us that "in New Orleans, Proposition 13 always existed." In 1979, a property tax surcharge that circumvented the normal channel of voter approval was challenged by the city's residents even though the surcharge was extremely low ($150 per parcel). Under

Table 2.2   Relative tax burdens, 1970–1975.

	1970		
City	Own-Source Revenues Per Capita	Income Per Capita	Per Capita Own-Source Revenues as a Percentage of Per Capita Income
Baltimore	$285.3	$2,876	9.9%
Dallas	159.3	3,697	4.3%
Des Moines	142.0	3,404	4.2%
Hartford	389.8	3,107	12.5%
Newark	300.8	2,492	12.1%
New Orleans	166.5	2,705	6.2%
Pittsburgh	165.5	3,071	5.4%
Seattle	180.7	4,052	4.5%
St. Louis	218.7	2,726	8.0%

such conditions, the property tax cannot be considered a safety valve to offset revenue shortfalls. In New Orleans, this inability or unwillingness to raise property tax rates, together with a high poverty rate (26.8 percent), create a poor environment to increase own-source revenues.

For Hartford and Newark, property taxes already have reached what must be considered an upper bound with their tax rates of over $50 per $1000 of fair market value. Hartford's property tax revenues per capita in 1977 exceeded $500 and Newark's approached $300, while the average for all cities over 25,000 was only $114 in that year (U.S. Department of Commerce, *City Government Finances* 1977). Hartford's high proportion of tax-exempt land (because of its status as state capital) exacerbates its precarious revenue position. Thirty-two percent of Newark's land base is tax-exempt (because of religious and public buildings) and the mill rate has more than doubled since 1973. High property tax rates suggest that to maintain service levels, alternative revenue sources must be found.

Pittsburgh, Baltimore, and St. Louis tax property at a fairly average rate (approximately $27 per $1000 of fair market value), and Dallas, Des Moines, and Seattle tax property at a very low rate (less than $15 per $1000 of fair market value). The volatility of the property tax issues, however, especially in the post-Proposition 13 era, renders increases in the tax rate difficult even in traditionally favorable (i.e., low tax) situations. Furthermore, property taxes, if increased beyond a tolerable threshold, may have the adverse effect (from the central city's perspective) of forcing outmigration (Tiebout 1956).

	1975		1970–1975
Own-Source Revenues Per Capita	Income Per Capita	Per Capita Own-Source Revenues as a Percentage of Per Capita Income	Relative Change in Tax Burden
$416.3	$4,330	9.6%	−3.0%
255.9	5,285	4.8%	11.6%
217.8	4,975	4.4%	4.8%
528.6	3,997	13.2%	5.6%
417.0	3,348	12.5%	3.3%
263.7	4,029	6.5%	4.8%
162.2	4,426	3.7%	−31.5%
293.6	5,800	5.1%	13.3%
344.0	4,006	8.6%	7.5%

Source: U.S. Department of Commerce, Bureau of the Census, *Government Finances.*

The relative tax burden[2] in each of the cities can be seen in table 2.2 where own-source revenue receipts are compared to income in per capita terms. The resulting ratios are useful for comparing across cities and time. First, there is wide divergence among cities. For 1975, the range of per capita tax was from a low of $162 (Pittsburgh) to a high of $529 (Hartford), with several cities (Des Moines, Dallas, Seattle) in the lower range, and several cities (especially Baltimore and Newark) in the higher range. The final column for 1975 data reveals that relative tax burdens continue to be most severe in Hartford, Newark, Baltimore, and St. Louis, in spite of the fact that the cities relatively unaffected by fiscal stress (Dallas and Seattle) have increased their own tax burdens (see last column).

Fiscal distress can also be measured by the degree to which a city relies on a particular revenue source. In table 2.3, we offer two measures of this: the reliance on property tax revenues as a proportion of own-source (tax and total) revenue; and the percentage of total revenue that comes from intergovernmental aid. Each of these measures offers insight into the relative dependence of localities on particular types of revenue.

The reliance on property taxes as own-source revenue is particularly relevant in the post–Proposition 13 era. The volatility of the issue of property taxes may offset the potential for using the property tax as a safety valve. The importance of this phenomenon increases with the degree of reliance on property taxes as a proportion of own-source revenue.

In the absence of local ability to raise revenue, intergovernmental aid becomes the means by which service levels are maintained. Aid from state

Table 2.3   Measures of budgetary stress.

City	(1) Mill Rate on Fair Market Value	(2) Ratio of Assessed/Fair Market Value	(3) Property Tax as Percentage of Own-Source Receipts (a)	(b)	(4) Intergovernmental Aid as Percentage of Total Revenues (c)	(d)
Baltimore	59.9	44.3%	55.0	44.7%	7.8%	58.1%
Dallas	10.4	100.0	44.6	35.4	22.3	24.5
Des Moines	13.5	100.0	60.3	43.3	14.7	27.0
Hartford	57.7	70.0	90.3	77.2	11.6	49.0
New Orleans	70.0	10.0*	21.8	16.5	21.8	32.5
Newark	58.8	100.0	62.4	56.6	11.4	67.2
Pittsburgh (land) (building)	55.0 27.5	50.0	40.9	39.9	16.0	23.1
Seattle	4.96	100.0	22.3	17.2	7.2	28.5
St. Louis	27.4	100.0	12.8	10.6	17.4	27.2

*With exemptions of the first $3,000 of assessed value for homeowners and the first $5,000 for veterans.
(a). Excluding current charges.
(b). Including current charges.
(c). Federal aid as a percentage of general revenues.
(d). Intergovernmental aid as a percentage of general revenues.
Sources: For columns 1 and 2: U.S. Department of Commerce, Bureau of the Census, *County and City Data Book* (1978).
For columns 3 and 4: U.S. Department of Commerce, Bureau of the Census, *City Government Finances, 1982–83.*

and federal agencies offsets the decline of central-city revenues. Many federal programs that dispense money to cities include a *poverty* or *need* index, designed specifically to measure fiscal stress. Anti-Recessionary Fiscal Assistance (ARFA), Local Public Works (LPW; both the 1976 and 1977 versions), Urban Development Action Grants (UDAG), and other grant programs were designed in part to aid cities experiencing difficulty in raising needed revenues. As a city becomes more and more unable to raise sufficient revenues, it increasingly relies on federal aid. Thus the more fiscally stressed a city is, the higher the reliance on federal aid.

A second set of indicators used in this study focuses on the broader structural components of fiscal stress. Population shifts, for example, can adversely affect a city's revenue base. If the population statistic shows a decline in the city's population (e.g., Seattle's decline of 12.6 percent) but the city retains those with a greater capacity to pay, (e.g., Seattle's high per capita income and low poverty rates), then the negative consequences of outmigration on the city's revenue-generating capacity may be offset. On the other hand, the negative effects can be exacerbated if rapid outmigration leaves the city with high-need, low-income individuals and a high poverty rate (e.g., Newark and New Orleans in this study). The measures of income, population change, and the poverty rate (table 2.4) provide useful information on the socioeconomic environment of fiscal stress.

Also included as indicators of structural fiscal stress are two measures of the economic base or growth of the city: manufacturing value added and manufacturing employment (both measured in terms of change over time). Gains in manufacturing employment, considered to be a high employment multiplier (North 1955; Richardson 1969; Miernyk 1976), indicate a growing economic advantage for firms to locate or expand in a particular city. Miernyk argues that manufacturing is "the most important component of an economy's export base. This consideration results from the high income and employment multipliers associated with manufacturing, an outcome of the high degree of interdependence between the manufacturing firms and the suppliers of their inputs" (1976, 24).

A number of important observations can be made with regard to the fiscal condition of the nine cities in this study based on the indicators. First, most central cities in our study have lost population over the fifteen-year period studied, 1960–75. The only exception is Dallas with an increase of 19.6 percent, a result in part of its continuing capacity to annex surrounding territory. Dramatic decreases are noted for St. Louis (31 percent), Pittsburgh (24 percent), and Newark (16 percent). The decreases for the other central cities were also substantial. Population decreases are not always reflective of shifts from the central city to fringe areas; they can also be from the metropolitan area in general. This was true of several cities in our sample (Newark, Pittsburgh, and St. Louis), and reflects regional shifts as much as intrametropolitan shifts.

Declines in manufacturing employment and value added in manufacturing, when coupled with declining population bases, forebode great difficulty in generating revenues. Among our sample cities, Hartford, Newark, St. Louis, and Seattle each lost more than one-fourth of their manufacturing employment between 1958 and 1972. The trends in most of these cities have not changed. The exception is Seattle, where economic success or failure is tied primarily to the aerospace industry. Data for 1976 and 1977 suggest that employment increased substantially in response to demand for new passenger jets (City of Seattle 1977, 18, 19). Thus, Seattle's loss in manufacturing employment did not have a lingering negative impact. In Baltimore, New Orleans, and St. Louis, losses of manufacturing employment were not merely sectoral shifts. Between 1970 and 1975, these cities lost, respectively, 8,600, 1,400, and 11,800 service sector jobs as well (Black 1981).

Dallas, on the other hand, was once again the big winner with a gain of some 41 percent in manufacturing employment; Des Moines also made a

Table 2.4   Indicators of capacity to increase own-source revenues.

City	(1) Percentage Change in Population (1960–1975)	(2) Central-City Income as Percentage of National Per Capita Income (1975)
Baltimore	−9.0%	94.7%
Dallas	+19.6	115.6
Des Moines	−7.1	108.8
Hartford	−5.1	87.4
New Orleans	−11.8	88.1
Newark	−16.8	73.2
Pittsburgh	−24.1	96.8
St. Louis	−31.1	87.6
Seattle	−12.6	126.8

modest gain. Although the implications of changes in sectoral employment may not be clear implications for total employment, it should be understood that employment and production shifts may occur within a city rather than necessarily within the regional or metropolitan area as a whole. For example, New Orleans, while experiencing a loss in manufacturing employment in the city, has experienced a gain in the suburban ring that more than offsets central-city losses.

Nathan and Fossett (1979) have calculated manufacturing value added for a sample of fifty cities. The mean increase for the period from 1972 to 1976 was 38.1 percent. In our sample of cities, only New Orleans, Des Moines, and Dallas exceeded that average. Newark showed the smallest increases during the period, with 18.9 percent, or less than one-half the average.

The income characteristics of the cities over time show that by 1975, Newark's income per capita ($3,348) was only three-fourths of national per capita income. Other cities in our study with income per capita of less than the national average include Hartford, St. Louis, New Orleans, Baltimore, and Pittsburgh. Although regional variations in the cost of

(3) Central-City Income as Per- centage of SMSA Per Capita Income (1975)	(4) Poverty Rate (1970)	(5) Percentage Change in Manufacturing Employment (1958–1972)	(6) Percentage Change in Per Capita Income (1960–1975)	(7) Percentage Change in Manufacturing Value Added (1972–1976)
86.6%	19.8%	−18.9%	132%	33.3%
107.4	13.4	+41.3	138	52.2
98.0	10.4	+5.7	117	NA
75.5	19.2	−50.4	90	NA
96.2	26.8	−2.1	132	42.7
59.3	25.6	−39.8	87	18.9
94.6	17.4	−3.9	129	25.0
84.9	23.7	−28.6	122	37.8
107.1	10.9	−33.0	130	37.2

Sources: For columns 1, 2, 3, 5 and 6: U.S. Department of Commerce, Bureau of the Census, *County and City Data Book* (various years)
For column 4: Personal communication with Data Systems and Statistics Division, Office of Management, Community Development and Planning, HUD. These poverty rates are based on 1970 census information and refined by HUD for purposes of distributing revenue to cities under GRS, UDAG, and ARFA programs.
For column 7: U.S. Department of Commerce, Bureau of the Census, *Annual Survey of Manufacturing* (1975), table 2.

living would alter (offset for some and augment for others) these disparities, the trends are consistent with other indications of fiscal stress. So, too, are the trends in relative intrametropolitan disparity. As Fossett and Nathan (1983, 67) note, "there was an increasing disparity in the concentration of urban problems in the 1960s. . . ." In some older cities even the surburban rings lost ground relative to the suburban rings of growing regions, which further increased intrametropolitan disparity (Fossett and Nathan 1983). Newark, for example, showed central-city per capita income to be only 59.3 percent of metropolitan per capita income in 1975. Hartford's figure was 75.5 percent. Interestingly, in Dallas and Seattle, central-city per capita income is higher than in their suburbs, which reflects the dynamism of these central cities.

Finally, socioeconomic trends are reflected in the growing numbers of central-city residents who exist below the poverty line. In Newark and New Orleans, these numbers are indeed startling: in 1970, more than 25 percent of all residents live in poverty (by HUD's definition). Not far behind was St. Louis with a poverty rate of 23.7 percent.

In the face of high property taxes, income disparities, and employment declines, intergovernmental aid often becomes the means by which service levels are maintained. Table 2.3 shows that in 1982 intergovernmental aid was 24.5 percent of Dallas's total general revenues; on the other hand, it comprised more than 40 percent of Baltimore's, Hartford's, and Newark's. In fact, Baltimore and Newark received more than half their revenues from intergovernmental aid. However, the figure for Baltimore must be viewed cautiously, because the city is responsible for some activities that normally are the province of the state. For example, Baltimore is the only city in our study that builds and maintains the interstate highway system that passes through it; this is a state activity elsewhere. Because of this, the high proportion of intergovernmental aid to Baltimore (58 percent in 1982) is not necessarily indicative of fiscal stress to the extent that it is in Newark. Intergovernmental aid to Newark in FY 1982 comprised over two thirds of total revenues.

We do not pretend to have a clear scale of relative fiscal stress for our nine cities. There are some clear ordinal characteristics to our qualitative measures, but we have consciously avoided assigning fixed quantitative rankings on some single index precisely because of the nuances of qualitative differences and our dissatisfaction with many studies (e.g., Touche Ross 1979) that have assigned ranking "scores" based on rather arbitrary and incomplete indices. Dallas, Des Moines, and Seattle possessed "good" capacities to augment own-source revenues compared with other cities examined; Baltimore, Pittsburgh, and St. Louis rated "fair"; and Hartford, Newark, and New Orleans fell in the "poor" category. Our discussion of the relative fiscal strains experienced in nine cities is intended to highlight several issues. First, stress is not a universal phenomenon for all municipalities; however, many municipalities are experiencing the effects of changing fiscal realities. Second, current manifestations of fiscal stress have historical roots in expanded service levels, changing socioeconomic climates, the implementation of intergovernmental programs, and the deeds and misdeeds of past management. Finally, and of greatest importance to us, the fiscal health or distress of cities can affect their budgetary choices, which in turn affect the level to which they build and maintain the infrastructure.

Much has been made of late about the prospects for urban revitalization (Blair and Nachmias 1979; Rosenthal 1980; Schill and Nathan 1983). Unfortunately, the evidence suggests that although particular cases of economic or residential revival may have occurred in specific cities or specific areas within cities, national trends in urban conditions for the 1980s have not changed appreciably, and in fact conditions generally have worsened (Fossett and Nathan, 1983). As one author notes, to premise public policy in declining cities on the prospect of urban revival is at best premature, and at worst unwarranted wishful thinking that could have negative consequences (Bahl 1981, 206–207).

The long-term issues of fiscal distress are not necessarily limited to cities experiencing such effects now. Weinstein and Clark (1981) argue that it is facile to presume that a city's present demographic and economic growth necessarily augurs well for the future; growth can impose financial burdens of its own. Although we argue that there are far greater disadvantages and potential negative consequences for presently declining, already fiscally stressed cities, we accept the possibility of a dismal future for cities currently experiencing economic prosperity and growth. In fact, as we will argue later in this chapter, fiscal stress may well have different impacts on different cities. We choose, therefore, to examine the consequences of fiscal stress for specific urban functions.

Scenario of Urban Options

How will a city respond to a gradual but appreciable decline in fiscal capacity? What choices or decisions can be made to deal with growing stress, especially considering the many conflicting claims on resources? Further, how has the public recognition of scarcity affected municipal performance?

Urban fiscal stress is deleterious to the long-run potential for cities to generate economic growth. The city treasury becomes the battlefield upon which departments fight for declining receipts. Urban governments experience increasing pressures to be more generous with their scarce resources in caring for the poor and indigent; but cities must also meet the basic requirements of the infrastructure so that jobs and people (the revenue base) will not disappear. These twin demands have exacerbated the fiscal tensions in many cities. The response of urban governments toward the latter type of commitment, i.e., EOC or developmental activities, generally has not been satisfactory for a number of years, even though the potential for devastating impacts is known (G. Peterson 1976).

The fiscal climate of recent years has altered the spending patterns of many localities dramatically. It is not clear, however, that the fiscal crisis has had much impact on lowering public expectations. No longer can it be assumed that expenditures for specific services will continue to increase or even to remain at historical levels. As Levine (1980) succinctly notes, officials are faced with tough decisions that require innovative solutions. Levine suggests that the following questions will be useful in guiding these management decisions: (1) What services and benefits are mandated? (2) What activities can be terminated? (3) What additional revenues can be raised? (4) What activities can be assigned to other service providers? (5) How can efficiency be improved? (6) Where can low-cost or no-cost labor be used? (7) Where can capital investments be substituted for labor expenses? (8) Where can information-gathering methods be installed and improved? (9) Where can demand be reduced and services be rationed? (10) What policies can help strengthen the economic base and promote economic development? (11) What arrangements can be made to identify and strengthen the leadership of this process? Faced with the new reality of fiscal scarcity, one possible response is to rely on the traditional revenue-raising alternative, raising taxes. However, political considerations and statutory proscriptions do not make this a truly viable alternative for many jurisdictions (Matz 1981). A second option is to misuse existing funds to accommodate gaps in the operating budget. Reallocating such fund sources as pension funds and abusing various debt mechanisms may provide a temporary solution to short-term needs. The value of such practices as long-run solutions to fiscal scarcity is, however, justifiably suspect (Clark and Ferguson 1983). Rather, the probable choices for the future are that "local governments will have to significantly increase productivity, draw down available surpluses, or seek alternative revenue sources" just to maintain current expenditure levels (Matz 1981, 142).

In addition to these revenue-related alternatives, there may have to be serious cutbacks in services, payrolls, and functional purviews. "Doing with less" strategies can imply reduced funding of those programs and services that are perceived to be least efficient; or can imply that funding will be allocated only to those programs and services considered to be most efficient, or at least highest on a city's priority list. Another strategy, clearly the main focus of the Reagan administration, is to solidify the public/private interface, which will lead to such practices as: privatization of public-sector services (e.g., contracting out, abdicating traditional responsibilities to the private sector), UDAGs, private leveraging, urban enterprise zones, and charitable contributions from the private sector (voluntarism) (Savas 1981). It may also be possible to generate revenue through divestiture of public properties and lease-back agreements (Colman 1983). Still another approach is to increase locational incentives for tax "ratables" through liberal use of industrial revenue bonds, through tax breaks in newly annexed areas (similar to urban enterprise zone options in eligible jurisdictions), or through transfer of development rights on existing underdeveloped (usually tax-exempt) structures and space. Current legislation pending in Washington, however, may limit the use of such debt instruments.

Two additional options for coping with fiscal stress are likely in the future. First, cities may combine divestiture of public services with a pay-as-you-go or user-charge approach. (Colman 1983). This approach combines the privatization of development activity with cutbacks on service-delivery management as an attempt to relate incidence to use (Savas 1981; Miller 1982). A final option may be to defer operating expenditures such as the maintenance of physical infrastructure, and to postpone capital investments on new infrastructure which will relieve the operating cost of debt repayment (Levine, Rubin, and Wolohojian 1981).

A survey of 100 cities conducted by the U.S. Conference of Mayors

(1982, 4) highlighted the choices facing cities, given the realities of fiscal distress and reduced federal spending: "The FY 82 budget cuts have caused an immediate budget adjustment by cities. A significant majority have already made decisions to increase taxes, lay off workers, postpone capital spending, and reduce services."

Sixty percent of their sample had already laid off workers and another thirteen percent responded that they would in the near future; 40 percent said that had raised or soon would raise taxes; 69 percent stated they already had or soon would raise service levels; and 63 percent had or soon would defer planned capital spending as a result of federal cuts in the first two rounds of the Reagan budget (U.S. Conference of Mayors 1982, 4–12). The city of Cincinnati, for example, has "adopted a policy of 'planned shrinkage' of its physical plant where possible—even turning down grants to concentrate its own funds on maintaining what it has" (*Newsweek*, 2 August 1982, 18).

Each of the strategies noted above involves real costs or problems for localities and their residents. For example, the options of increasing property tax burdens or diversification involve both the historical problems noted earlier and the institutional and political problems of limitation policies or their prospect. There is some evidence that one factor motivating limitation policies is a desire to shift tax burdens to the state level. That this outcome of limitation movements has occurred is evident, for example, in New Jersey, where Governor Kean's "lean look" was accompanied in January 1983 by increases in the state income tax for some wage earners (Moore and Beer 1984).

Proponents of "planned shrinkage" of services and service delivery argue that cutbacks need not involve a change in the quality of service. Instead, constraints are likely to lead to more productive and effective use of services. They argue that recent years have seen a burgeoning public payroll, due not merely to increased work loads, but also to inefficient staffing, inherent bureaucratic tendencies toward maximizing budgets, monopoly on certain services, and public employee control over implementing policy and making policy decisions (Savas 1981; Auletta 1975). Prospects of increased scarcity have already led to some innovative proposals for money management. New Jersey, Massachusetts, and other states have tried to create statewide "infrastructure banks" that would create self-financing capital investment funds, encourage the more efficient use of federal grant monies, and prioritize projects statewide. Important political hurdles and the rigid nature of federal grant programs have blocked progress in creating such mechanisms, but the need for such efforts remains (Moore and Beer 1984).

However, not everyone agrees that increased management efficiency will be sufficient to prevent service delivery changes. As one group of scholars noted, if employment in public services is reduced, there is a high probability that "the most dependent segments of the population will receive lower quantities and/or qualities of public services" (Bahl, Jump, and Schroeder 1978, 33). Although cities that reduce service levels generally improve their fiscal conditions, from an equity or political perspective this may not be a desirable trade-off.

The likelihood of an increased public/private interface in the financing and developmental functions of city governments has become a reality of the 1980s (Fosler and Berger 1982; Bearse 1982). Under President Carter, and particularly in his 1978 *National Urban Policy Report* (U.S. President 1978), a recognition of and a direction to the new partnership were evident. As noted in a recent National Research Council report: "These new attitudes about public-private relationships suggest a different urban policy strategy in which the private sector plays a central role and in which public policy is closely examined for its impact on the local business economy. If public investment and regulation policy can reduce costs to businesses and consumers, then public resources can be husbanded to deal primarily with these problems that cannot be addressed by the market economy" (1981, 69).

Even if the new leveraging of private investment does stimulate economic development activity, it remains questionable whether social needs will be met and human capital investments will be forthcoming. However, such issues as leveraging, fiscal scarcity, and prioritization of needs raise questions that are of particular relevance to this study: Will the quality of physical infrastructure be affected by fiscal choices? Will the push for expenditure reductions affect maintenance and capital expenditures? In addition, one might ask whether changing conditions in the bond market, and the desire to reduce debt burdens will contribute to declines in capital investment (Moore and Pagano 1982).

It has been argued that maintenance is often the first item in the public agenda to be cut under conditions of stress (Peterson 1978; Grossman 1977; Kain 1978). As the President's 1978 *National Urban Policy Report* states: "Failure to keep up a city's infrastructure is often a politically less sensitive action than cuts in the workforce" (U.S. President 1978, 94). Another common practice is the deferral of spending. The prevalence of this practice in the last decade has led many to predict a dismal future for the nation's capital stock. Choate and Walter highlight the effect of delay by suggesting that "Time is, indeed, money. . . . Financing delay has become a major levy on available monies for public works. About 20 percent ($16 billion) of the nation's annual public works appropriations are now used for such financing—a major and unnecessary waste of shrinking public capital" (1981, 40). Problems of delay may, at times, be unavoidable, but the consequences may be severe. Delayed projects often become unaffordable due to inflation and the high costs of borrowing.

Like construction and investment delay, maintenance deferral can be prohibitively more expensive in the long run. During the 1970s, repair and maintenance activities declined precipitously, resulting in a deteriorated condition of urban capital stock. As the severe repair needs of the Interstate Highway System attest, and as is now recognized in national policy, maintenance deferral can be very costly: "In 1971, $1 million would rebuild 6.4 miles of highway. Today, it rebuilds just 1.5 miles" (*Newsweek*, 2 August 1982, 15). Yet, from the perspective of cities, there is little choice. Most choose to delay, defer, reduce, or eliminate, and deal with the consequences later. What is not clear is that this response has been unique to fiscally stressed cities, nor is it clear that this response has been uniform for all functions.

Fiscal Condition and Infrastructure Expenditures

One measure of the condition of public facilities is the amount spent to maintain facilities, to expand existing capacity, or to replace worn out or obsolete facilities. For the nine case studies reported here, data were collected on actual maintenance and capital expenditures, corrected for inflation, for from ten to twenty-one years (1957–1977), depending on availability (see appendix 1 for a more complete statement on the methodology of this study).

In this section, we examine the degree to which fiscal stress has affected both maintenance (an operating budget concern) and capital (a capital budget concern) expenditures. Several issues are of relevance. Do cities that perform many functions experience greater burdens, and do different financial burdens translate into different maintenance patterns? Does greater fiscal stress result in lower levels of maintenance? Does fiscal stress affect patterns of capital expenditure?

It is often suggested that poor performance in financing maintenance and capital expenditures is a consequence of the number of activities for which a city assumes responsibility. For example, Dye and Garcia argue that "the most important determinant of municipal taxing and spending is the functional scope of city government" (1978, 12). In other words, cities with broader functional scopes are more likely to experience greater fiscal difficulties than those with narrow scopes. The implication is that expenditures will decline as functional scope diminishes, which will make cities fiscally healthier so that they can better perform their remaining functions, such as maintenance. This is a common justification for the metropolitanization of service districts, or for attempts to remove certain functional responsibilities from a city.

However, our data do not support this perspective. Using a modified version of Liebert's (1979) count of city functional scope, table 2.5 compares functional scope and maintenance patterns for our "sample" cities. In this analysis, scope does not appear to have much bearing in explaining maintenance trends. Baltimore, with one of the broadest-scope governments, increased constant dollar sewer maintenance expenditures over the twenty-one year period, but street and bridge maintenance dropped. Pittsburgh, with one of the narrowest functional scopes of the nine cities, witnessed declines for both of its city-owned functions (streets and bridges, and water). On the other hand, two other narrow-scope governments, Dallas and Des Moines, registered increases in maintenance outlays for the city-owned water systems. Dallas experienced a decline in street and bridge maintenance and an increase in sewer maintenance, and Des Moines experienced a fairly negligible change in both street and bridge maintenance and sewer maintenance. Seattle, the other narrow-scope government, decreased outlays for streets and bridges and the city's sewage-collection system, but water-system maintenance remained relatively stable. The other broad-scope governments appear not to have performed well, but the data are too inconclusive to make inferences about the effects of functional scope on maintenance outlays.

Maintenance Expenditures and Fiscal Stress   A more careful examination of maintenance trends in the nine cities is provided by tables 2.6, 2.7, and 2.8, which present maintenance expenditures for each of the major functional categories of infrastructure examined in this study. For purposes of readability, the data are presented in groups of five years (six years for the first group), and average expenditures for these periods appear in parentheses under each period.

Table 2.6 presents data on street and bridge maintenance expenditures. The patterns evident here, particularly in the last time period, clearly show a dramatic decline in maintenance for streets and bridges. Although there are differences in expenditure patterns across cities in earlier periods, which merit discussion, the uniform declines in more recent years are frightening. Between 1957 and 1977, constant dollar expenditures declined in all cities; in some cities (Hartford and Newark) these declines were as much as 68 percent. Even in the best case (Des Moines), declines over time were substantial, particularly in recent years. Note that in the 1963–67 period, three cities increased constant dollar maintenance expenditures, and five decreased outlays. In the 1968–72 period, four cities increased outlays and four decreased. But in the last period, 1973–77, only one city did not decrease maintenance expenditures (Seattle). This last period is somewhat surprising in light of expectations that federal general revenue sharing (GRS) funds (analyzed in chapter 3) might have contributed to an overall improvement in maintenance outlays. On the other hand, this last

Table 2.5   Functional scope and constant-dollar maintenance expenditures.

	Common Functions[1]	Increase (+) or Decrease (−) in Twenty-one-year Trend in Maintenance Expenditures[2]				
		Streets and Bridges	City-Owned Water	City-Owned Sewer	Special District Water	Special District Sewer
Baltimore	8	−	NA	+		
Dallas	4	−	+	+		
Des Moines	4	0	+	0		
Hartford	8	−			+[3]	+[3]
Newark	7	−	NA	− (sewage collection)		0 (sewage treatment)
New Orleans[3]	6	0	0	−		
Pittsburgh	4	−	−[3]	0 (sewage collection)		+ (sewage treatment)
St. Louis	8	−	−			NA
Seattle	4	−	0	− (sewage collection)		NA (sewage treatment)

NA = Data not available in comparable form.

1. Derived from Liebert (1979); eight is the highest possible number of common functions in Liebert's table.

2. "0" indicates a twenty-one-year change of no more than ± 10 percent; " + " indicates a twenty-one-year increase of more than 10 percent; " − " indicates a twenty-one-year decrease of more than 10 percent.

3. Data for 1967–1977 only.

Source: Field data.

period (1973–1977) corresponds to financially disastrous years for many cities. The question arises whether we witness this decline in maintenance only among fiscally stressed cities. The answer is clearly a resounding "no," although there appears to be some relationship between degree of fiscal stress and the intensity of decline. Thus, fiscal stress is important as a constraining parameter; it does not, however, appear to be a cause of neglect.

On an individual city basis, Hartford and Newark witnessed the most dramatic decline in street and bridge maintenance expenditures, plummeting over 65 percent during the twenty-one-year period. St. Louis and Seattle decreased expenditures by about 20 to 25 percent during the same period. Baltimore, Dallas, and Pittsburgh diminished outlays by approximately 20 percent, and Des Moines declined very slightly.

Table 2.6   Percentage change in maintenance expenditures for streets and bridges (in thousands of 1972 dollars).

	1957–1962	1963–1967	1968–1972	1973–1977	1957–1977
Baltimore	— ($6627)*	−12.4% ($5806)	+1.1% ($5872)	−12.95% ($5111)	−22.9%
Dallas	— ($3608)	+18.7% ($4281)	+5.1% ($4500)	−36.6% ($2853)	−20.9%
Des Moines	— ($2055)	+79.9% ($3697)	−38.6% ($2271)	−13.4% ($1967)	−4.3%
Hartford	— ($ 389)	−53.98% ($ 179)	+79.3% ($ 321)	−61.99% ($ 122)	−68.6%
Newark	— ($1992)	−27.3% ($1449)	−16.4% ($1211)	−46.1% ($ 653)	−67.2%
New Orleans	NA	NA	— ($2575)	−5.9% ($2422)	−5.9%
Pittsburgh	— ($5172)	−5.8% ($4872)	−21.9% ($3807)	0.0% ($3811)	−26.3%
St. Louis	— ($4016)	−21.2% ($3165)	+19.1% ($3770)	−26.9% ($2757)	−31.3%
Seattle	— ($1498)	+12.7% ($1688)	−37.5% ($1055)	+4.5% ($1102)	−26.4%

*Figures in parentheses correspond to average annual expenditures for that time period.
Note: For converting to 1972 dollars, we used the Skilled Labor Index from *Engineering News-Record* (1978). New York's indexes were substituted for Newark's. In two cases (Des Moines and Hartford) we used surrogate city measures from the U.S. Bureau of Labor Statistics (1957–1977). New Haven's indexes were used as surrogates for Hartford's; Des Moines's indexes were available until 1975, after which Omaha's indexes were used.
Source: Field data.

The expenditure patterns for sewer and water maintenance differ significantly from street and bridge expenditures, even where all three activities are provided by the city government (which is the case for Baltimore, Dallas, Des Moines and New Orleans). From available data in tables 2.7 and 2.8, there was only one case of a dramatic decline in water or sewer maintenance expenditures, and that is Pittsburgh's maintenance expenditure for the water system, down by more than 60 percent between 1967 and 1977. The decline in Pittsburgh, however, is primarily the result of changes in accounting practices on the one hand, and of the failure to count Comprehensive Employment and Training Act (CETA) employees on the other. Thus, the decline in Pittsburgh, if it happened at all, was not substantial. In the other cities, there was not as much decline as in street and bridge

Table 2.7   Percentage change in maintenance expenditures
for water systems (in thousands of 1972 dollars).

	1957–1962	1963–1967	1968–1972	1973–1977	1957–1977
Baltimore	— ($1780)*	+28.3% ($2284)	NA	NA	NA
Dallas	— ($3587)	+12.1% ($4020)	+1.0% ($4061)	+18.7% ($4820)	+34.4%
Des Moines	— ($ 728)	+22.5% ($ 892)	+18.2% ($1054)	+4.5% ($1101)	+51.2%
Hartford	— ($ 971)	NA	— ($1239)	+9.5% ($1357)	+39.8%
Newark	NA	NA	NA	NA	NA
New Orleans	NA	NA	— ($1738)	−7.4% ($1609)	NA
Pittsburgh	NA	NA	— ($1849)	−60.4% ($ 732)	NA
St. Louis	— ($2449)	+2.7% ($2515)	−7.1% ($2337)	−8.1% ($2125)	−13.2%
Seattle	NA	NA	— ($1689)	−10.4% ($1514)	NA

*Figures in parentheses correspond to average annual expenditures for that time period.
Note: For converting to 1972 dollars, we used the Skilled Labor Index from *Engineering News-Record* (1978). New York's indexes were substituted for Newark's. In two cases (Des Moines and Hartford) we used surrogate city measures from the U.S. Bureau of Labor Statistics (1957–1977). New Haven's indexes were used as surrogates for Hartford's; Des Moines's indexes were available until 1975, after which Omaha's indexes were used.
Source: Field data.

maintenance outlays. Furthermore, special districts did not perform significantly differently from city-owned water and sewer services (see table 2.5 for identification of these). The only non–city-owned water district, Hartford's, increased maintenance outlays over the study period. City-owned water systems increased maintenance expenditures in Dallas and Des Moines, decreased outlays in Pittsburgh and St. Louis, and remained unchanged in New Orleans and Seattle. Table 2.8 shows that expenditure trends for sewer maintenance increased in Baltimore and Dallas (city owned), decreased in New Orleans and Des Moines (city owned), and remained unchanged for Pittsburgh's sewer collection system (city owned). Close examination reveals several trends. Some activities do fare poorly in terms of expenditures over time. This is clearly the case for maintenance of streets and bridges. On the other hand, even fiscally stressed cities maintain

Table 2.8 Percentage change in maintenance expenditures
for sewer systems (in thousands of 1972 dollars).

	1957–1962	1963–1967	1968–1972	1973–1977	1957–1977
Baltimore	— ($1217)*	0.0% ($1216)	+174.8% ($3341)	+39.8% ($4670)	+283.7%
Dallas	— ($2045)	+14.9% ($2349)	+9.0% ($2561)	+12.8% ($2889)	+41.3%
Des Moines	— ($1241)	+8.1% ($1342)	−6.6% ($1254)	−10.5% ($1122)	−9.6%
Hartford	NA	NA	— ($ 757)	+19.9% ($ 908)	NA
Newark	— ($2572)	−6.9% ($2413)	−4.3% ($2310)	+19.9% ($2770)	+7.7%
New Orleans	NA	NA	— ($1303)	−13.2% ($1131)	NA
Pittsburgh	— ($ 640)	+68.9% ($1081)	−3.3% ($1045)	+29.7% ($1355)	+111.7%
St. Louis	NA	NA	NA	NA	NA
Seattle**	— ($1200)	+6.2% ($1274)	−32.8% ($ 856)	+4.7% ($ 896)	−25.3%

*Figures in parentheses correspond to average annual expenditures for that time period.
**Does not include maintenance of the treatment plant; only of the collection system.
Note: For converting to 1972 dollars, we used the Skilled Labor Index from *Engineering News-Record* (1978). New York's indexes were substituted for Newark's. In two cases (Des Moines and Hartford) we used surrogate city measures from the U.S. Bureau of Labor Statistics (1957–1977). New Haven's indexes were used as surrogates for Hartford's; Des Moines's indexes were available until 1975, after which Omaha's indexes were used.
Source: Field data.

water and sewer systems reasonably well. Thus, although degree of fiscal stress has caused some differences in maintenance across cities, the pattern of these differences depends upon which functional activity one examines. Furthermore, where the function "sits" (i.e., city-owned versus special district) does not much affect whether maintenance is carried out adequately. We speculate that it may be that differences in financing mechanisms or bases (user fees as opposed to funds from the general fund, for example) can explain differences in levels of maintenance. Lack of competition for the use of funds in water and sewer activities, whether a separate authority exists for these activities or not, means that operating funds for routine maintenance are more likely to be made when city functions are financed through user fees, rate changes are seen as technical responses, and decision making is perceived in less politically volatile terms. This means that such functions are often treated as if they were somewhat independent, (regardless of whether they are part of the city budget), and are spared severe cutbacks.

It would seem, then, that fiscal stress may indeed exacerbate decision-making tensions in the operating budget. However, the impact of fiscal stress on maintenance expenditures across different functions is less clear. This relative insulation from the political volatility that comes with fiscal stress means that maintenance expenditures are often not as severely affected.

Capital Outlays and Fiscal Stress   When capital expenditures are included in the analysis, no consistent trend is visible. Tables 2.9 through 2.12 present actual capital expenditures for each of the major functional areas of infrastructure in this study. Again, the data are presented in groups of five years (six years for the first group), and each column lists average annual expenditures for these periods. Note that capital expenditures for all functional activities tend to be "lumpy" over the twenty-one-year period. For example, in the case of Des Moines the percentage change between the first and second period for bridges exceeds 2,000 percent; yet between the second and third period, the percentage change declines by more than 50 percent (table 2.9). Therefore, tables 2.9 through 2.12 do not present percentage changes.

Tables 2.9 and 2.10 provide data on capital expenditures for streets and bridges for the nine cities. Most apparent in these tables is the very different absolute levels of expenditures for these functions among cities. As opposed to maintenance expenditure patterns, most of our cities do not show dramatic decreases in capital expenditures over the twenty-one-year period, with the exception of St. Louis, where decline has been dramatic. Between the first and second periods, only Baltimore and St. Louis show declines in average annual capital expenditures, and growing cities such as Dallas, Des Moines, and Seattle show substantial increases. The remaining cities show fairly stable expenditure patterns. In the 1968–1972 period, Baltimore and St. Louis again show substantial cutbacks in capital expenditures, but other cities either maintained or increased existing expenditure levels. Interestingly, the last period shows several trends that are contrary to expectations that relate degree of fiscal stress to capital expenditures. Fiscally stressed cities either increased or maintained patterns of capital expenditures, and Des Moines and Seattle showed declines.

The implication would seem to be that factors other than fiscal stress account for changes in levels of capital expenditures for streets and bridges. In Dallas, physical expansion clearly accounts for the dramatic changes between the first and last periods. In some other cities, mature street

Table 2.9   Capital expenditures for bridge systems
(in thousands of 1972 dollars).[1]

	1957–1962	1963–1967	1968–1972	1973–1977
Baltimore[2]	—	—	—	—
Dallas	544.6	867.5	547.2	213.1
Des Moines	122.9	2922.9	1261.3	940.0
Hartford[2]	—	—	—	—
Newark	0	2.2	163.1	127.8
New Orleans	NA	NA	19.3	18.9
Pittsburgh	177.3	63.6	946.1	262.7
St. Louis	2231.9	1026.5	40.8	620.4
Seattle[2]	—	—	—	—

1. For converting to 1972 dollars, indexes were drived from the Building Cost Index,
Engineering News-Record (1978). Figures in columns are for average annual expenditures.
2. Included in streets.
Source: Field data.

systems require lower expansion (although perhaps higher levels of replacement), and this is reflected in expenditure levels.

The data for sewer systems (table 2.11) show similarly irregular patterns. Across the twenty-one year period some of our most fiscally stressed cities have provided remarkably stable capital funding (Baltimore, for example). Others have increased annual expenditures dramatically (Newark and New Orleans), or have fluctuated (St. Louis). The data once more suggest that the presence of fiscal stress does not determine expenditure patterns.

Only in water systems (table 2.12) do we note any systematic decline in capital expenditures over the twenty-one-year period. All cities expended less at the end of the time frame, regardless of the presence of fiscal stress or the type of funding source (for example, special districts in the case of Hartford).

Total Outlays and Fiscal Stress   In capital expenditures overall, with the exception of those for water systems, a generally downward trend was perceived in only a few instances, and even in those cases, the decline was less severe and of less duration than declines in maintenance expenditures. Due in part to the long-term neglect of maintenance, local public works personnel characterized unmet needs as great. With the exceptions of Dallas and Des Moines, the cities in our study experienced the problems of maintenance declines. As a result of past neglect, needs have become new capital expenditures. In Dallas and Des Moines, infrastructure was in generally good condition, maintenance outlays had either increased or

Table 2.10   Capital expenditures for street systems (in thousands of 1972 dollars).[1]

	1957–1962	1963–1967	1968–1972	1973–1977
Baltimore[2]	60,252.3	49,545.2	27,735.7	66,890.6
Dallas	9,419.1	20,611.0	17,986.0	24,466.0[3]
	9,963.7	21,478.5	18,533.2	24,679.1
Des Moines	1,588.6	3,517.9	4,618.4	3,361.0
	1,711.5	6,440.8	5,879.7	4,301.0
Hartford[2]	78.0	248.2	441.6	1,197.1
Newark	234.2	214.3	1,200.6	886.4
		216.5	1,363.7	1,014.2
New Orleans	NA	NA	6,815.5	7,221.3
			6,834.8	7,240.2
Pittsburgh	4,093.1	5,222.1	4,483.9	4,995.1
	4,270.4	5,285.7	5,430.0	5,257.8
St. Louis	4,868.7	4,342.9	748.5	613.5
	7,100.6	5,369.4	789.3	1,233.9
Seattle[2]	8,804.4	9,448.6	9,333.3	7,273.1

1. For converting to 1972 dollars, indexes were derived from the Building Cost Index, *Engineering News-Record* (1978). Figures in columns are for average annual expenditures.

2. Includes bridges. In the cases of remaining cities, second number is combined street and bridge capital expenditures. Unlike other cities, Baltimore receives federal interstate highway funds.

3. Estimated rather than actual.

Source: Field data.

remained stable, and new capital investments were in the planning stages to meet increased needs due to growth. However, it is not clear that these trends are continuing. More recently than our 1979 field work, even the stable cities seem to be feeling the impact of fiscal tightness. For example, the U.S. Conference of Mayors in a recent study reported that Des Moines postponed a major sewer project (1982, 12).

Conditions of fiscal solvency and infrastructure generally would have been even worse than described above had it not been for federal programs. As noted in table 2.1, federal capital grants are a substantial portion of total state and local capital outlays. Throughout the 1960s and 1970s, the federal contribution represented more than one-quarter (and more recently as much as 41 percent) of total state and local capital outlays.

Summary

Our argument here is neither tautological nor trivial. We do not simply conclude that fiscally stressed cities spend less because they have insufficient revenues. Although there is some relationship between fiscal stress and

Table 2.11   Capital expenditures for sewer systems
(in thousands of 1972 dollars).[1]

	1957–1962	1963–1967	1968–1972	1973–1977
Baltimore	13,041.9	6,579.1	5,122.8	15,597.7
Dallas	5,306.2	7,048.0	7,548.2	11,738.3
Des Moines	536.1	1,574.3	1,065.1	1,467.0
Hartford	NA	NA	14,100.0	5,439.2
Newark				
Treatment	426.5	671.5	4,458.0	4,607.1
Collection	147.6	3,978.8	1,754.7	110.3
New Orleans	NA	2,056[2]	4,319.0	9,797.5
Pittsburgh				
Treatment	NA	NA	11,119.3[3]	1,092.4
Collection	519.6	446.2	697.6	490.5
St. Louis	348.6	13,155.5	18,312.2	6,039.5
Seattle				
Treatment	NA	28,394.3	11,660.9	7,193.8
Collection	7,104.8	4,942.8	14,269.0[3]	7,086.7

1. For converting to 1972 dollars, indexes were derived from those of the U.S. Environmental Protection Agency (1977). Figures in columns are for average annual expenditures.
2. Data for 1967 only.
3. Data for 1969–1972.
Source: Field data.

spending patterns, conscious decisions are made by city officials; cuts are not automatic and uncontrollable. Therefore, it is not uncommon for even the most fiscally stressed city to increase spending, even as its fiscal base deteriorates (based on current dollars).

We argue that much of the writing on the crisis of urban infrastructure overplays the responsibility of fiscal stress in the neglect of maintenance activities. Declines in maintenance expenditures occurred at the same time that total expenditures in the operating budget increased. For example, between fiscal year 1967–68 and fiscal year 1976–77, Baltimore increased total current dollar city expenditures by 163 percent, Dallas by 144 percent, Des Moines by 126 percent, Hartford by 198 percent, New Orleans by 113 percent, Newark by 123 percent, Pittsburgh by 90 percent, St. Louis by 120 percent, and Seattle by 107 percent. Had maintenance expenditures increased at the same rate as total city expenditures, current dollar maintenance expenditures would have been considerably greater. (These data are graphically presented in chapter 3.) Indeed, except for one city, the rates of increase in maintenance expenditures for streets and bridges were significantly less than for total city outlays; except for two cities,

Table 2.12   Capital expenditures for water systems
(in thousands of 1972 dollars).[1]

	1957–1962	1963–1967	1968–1972	1973–1977
Baltimore	28,110.5	14,271.9	3,443.6	4,450.1
Dallas	17,412.6	17,896.6	13,525.7	8,896.8
Des Moines	1,504.8[2]	469.3	1,235.0	1,056.2
Hartford	3,650.6[3]	NA	8,147.1	1,722.9
Newark	3,289.9	1,808.1	700.6	356.6
New Orleans	NA	2,503.5[4]	2,497.1	2,138.2
Pittsburgh	3,412.4	1,839.7	1,575.2	1,482.0
St. Louis	12,144.8[5]	4,146.0	2,250.6	3,473.1
Seattle	9,216.0	4,527.8	4,489.3	2,733.8

1. For converting to 1972 dollars, indexes were derived from those of the U.S. Environmental Protection Agency (1957–1977). Figures in columns are for average annual expenditures.
2. Data for 1958–1962.
3. Data for 1957 and 1962 only.
4. Data for 1967 only.
5. Data for 1960–1962 only.
Source: Field data.

the rates of increase for water system maintenance expenditures were less than the rates of total city outlays; and the rates of increase for sewer maintenance expenditures were less in four of the nine cities. Clearly, other activities were absorbing larger and larger portions of the budget. We will show that budget competition and the growth of soc responsibilities are clearly the culprits.

We turn in the next chapter to the role that federal grants have had in contributing to the current infrastructure crisis.

3. The Budgetary Process and the Impact of Federal Grants

Fiscal stress is not an adequate explanation for declining urban maintenance and capital outlays. The point is not that cities are unaffected by
fiscal stress, but rather that declines in maintenance and capital expenditures have been widespread for cities of varying fiscal conditions. In this
chapter, we explore the role of changes in the federal grants system in
contributing to the infrastructure problem.

We examine three impacts of federal grants. First, we evaluate the impacts
of federal grants on the capital budgetary process. Has the presence of
grants altered how cities fund capital programs or budget for capital expenditures? Second, we discuss the existence and impact of antimaintenance
provisions in federal grant programs for infrastructure. Have federal programs affected how cities finance maintenance activities in the operating
budget, and, if so, how? Third, we explore the effects of local governmental reliance on federal grant programs for their infrastructure programs. Has
reliance on federal grants encouraged local governments to make investment decisions in capital programs that they otherwise would not have
made?

The Budgetary Impacts of Federal Capital Grants

The process of capital budget allocation is a much neglected area of the
public budgeting and finance literature. Most studies focus on outputs or
expenditure levels, and not on the process or the behavior of capital budget
makers. With the exception of Wildavsky's classic study (1964), which
treats the federal budget as unified (i.e., both capital and operating items
are taken together), most budgetary process studies and models ignore the
capital budget (Crecine 1969; Larkey 1979; and Danziger 1976). What
may account for this omission is the "lumpiness" of capital outlays as
contrasted with fairly small or incremental changes in operating budget
outlays. For example, according to *City Government Finances* (U.S. Depart-

ment of Commerce 1957–83), Hartford's capital expenditures in fiscal year (FY) 73 were $26.0 million, in FY 74 they nearly doubled to $40.8 million, then declined to $26.0 million and $21.6 million in FY 75 and FY 76; Baltimore's capital outlays between FY 69 and FY 74 fluctuated from $97.1 million to $152.0 million, and then in FY 76 increased to $277 million from $194.7 million in FY 75. Even a growing city, Dallas, demonstrated a lumpiness to its capital outlays by declining from $64.0 to $58.9 million in FY 70 and FY 71, then increasing to $85.1 million in FY 74 and declining to $54.6 million in FY 76. Thus, this lumpy trend in city capital outlays is common to many cities. However this phenomenon does not proscribe incremental analysis. We argue, however, that if the federal contribution to capital projects is removed, an incremental analysis can apply. We begin with a theory of the capital budget process and bureaucratic behavior within the process, and proceed to an evaluation of the impact of federal grants.

Theory of Capital Budgeting

The first step in the capital budgeting process involves the determination by agencies or departments of their needs (see figure 3.1). These *needs assessments* are developed and rank-ordered on the basis of formal or informal decision criteria, such as a project's enhancement of residents' safety, its economic development impact, and whether it maintains the existing system or expands it. For example, street departments often rank resurfacing projects ahead of new construction projects (e.g., construction of a minor street). After an internal review to place some constraints on the total list, these projects are then sent to the central budget office. Budget officers, or capital budget officers, then review the project list in light of their revenue projections for the year (which rely to a considerable extent on existing and future tax rates), and the specific agency's share of the total capital budget. The former consideration assumes that as long as the (property, income, etc.) tax rate is known or knowable, revenue projections can give a "ballpark figure" to work with and within which to review projects. The latter concern ensures that no one agency will receive all capital funds or an inequitable amount. Rather, the apportionment of capital funds to agencies is predicated on a "fair share" concept similar to Wildavsky's (1964) notion.

When the budget officers have completed their *financial assessment*, they send a revised list of projects back to the agency. The agency continues to revise the list of projects and resubmit it to the budget office until the agency and the budget office reach an agreement. The resulting document becomes the official capital budget, which is either approved or modified by city council. Of course, when the duration of a capital project extends

Figure 3.1   The process of capital budget allocation.

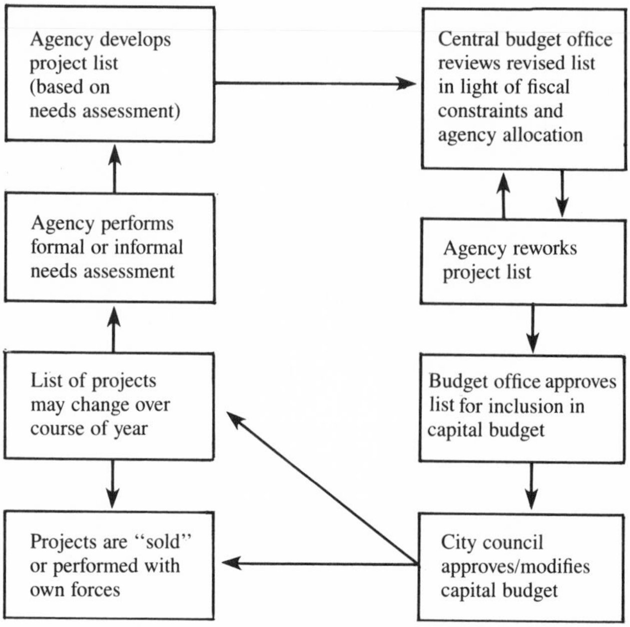

over more than one year (e.g., construction of a convention center), the flow of funds to cover that ongoing project is usually not debated by budget officials except in extreme cases when cost revisions make the project unaffordable (e.g., New York's Westway or third water tunnel). Then too, during the course of a budget year, the project list can change. Emergency projects (e.g., bridge collapse) can supplant "approved" projects, projects can advance to "ready" status, projects can be delayed, or projects may require additional funds resulting in budgetary modifications elsewhere (see Hoskins 1984).

The capital allocation process operates within a very complex environment with many actors defining the context within which capital decisions result. Bureaucratic behavior in proposing capital projects for funding is constrained primarily by three interrelated factors: (1) the incremental nature of public budgeting, (2) the financial capacity of the local government to fund any given set of projects, and (3) the willingness of the actors to divert a portion of the city's wealth to the public fisc.

We begin by assuming that bureaucrats attempt to maximize the total amount of funds to be spent by them (or their agencies) in any given year for at least two reasons (see Wolf 1979; Drucker 1973). First, the prestige of a government agency is reflected in the amount of funds that the city, or more appropriately the city council, is willing to commit to that agency. The problems and priorities addressed by budgetary outlays reflect underlying community values. If community values favor a particular agency, it will receive more revenue for its capital projects, or, to put it another way, more of its needs will be addressed. The prestige, importance, reputation, and indeed, power of the agency — as well as of the bureaucrats themselves — are therefore affected by the amount of funds the agency receives. Second, the physical needs of an agency always exceed available resources. Capital facilities wear out or become obsolete and need to be replaced or reconstructed, and changes in citizen preferences require new facilities (e.g., feeder streets to highways). For both of these reasons, the agency tries to augment its resource base by capturing a greater amount of public capital funds.

However, the very complex, interactive capital budgetary process acts as a check on the agency's behavior. Limits on the city's ability to fund the capital budget and the competition for funds among agencies restrain any one agency's attempts to address all its needs and optimize its power/ prestige position. The actors who play this watchdog role are the budget and/or finance officers and city council. Budget and finance officers control behavior by scrutinizing spending so that budgetary requests do not exceed projected revenues. Policy makers (city council, in particular) have an added restraining function: they hold down tax rates. Although policy makers would also like growth in the budget, both to increase their own prestige and to allow them to address the city's needs, raising taxes to accomplish these objectives is usually politically undesirable. Traditional revenue sources for a city's General Fund, especially property and income taxes, are viewed negatively by taxpayers, and moves to increase such taxes create hostility toward policy makers. The result of holding the line on taxes is that spending cannot increase — depending on the elasticities of the taxes which finance the General Fund. Thus, the behavior of bureaucrats is constrained by the attempt on the one hand to hold down city taxes, and on the other by the drive to shape the activities and direction of the city through expanding the budget. In the past, these contradictory tendencies have sometimes been reconciled (temporarily) through postponing payment (and tax hikes) by borrowing from future earnings and spending more today (a larger budget). New York City's near-default was in part the result of its attempt to enlarge the budget without raising taxes by borrowing money for current operating expenses. Since the near-default, short-term borrowing has been severely restricted for such purposes. Indeed, it is highly unlikely that New York's example will help in resolving the policy makers' attempts to both spend more and simultaneously hold down general taxes.

In order to meet these twin restraints, in the past few years, cities have begun to tap new, "creative" financing mechanisms, which often involve the use of industrial development revenue bonds, sale/lease-back arrangements, etc. (Hamilton 1983; Petersen and Hough 1983). The reasons for the recent popularity of such financing techniques are (1) that many cities have already imposed what residents consider to be an excessive tax burden, which has resulted in many cases in tax and expenditure limitations, closing the door to traditional methods of generating revenues, and (2) that fiscally stressed cities, regardless of the tax burden, need to find other revenues in order to maintain existing levels of city services. Creative financing is attractive to policy makers and budget officials because it can generate needed revenues without increasing the tax burden on residents.

But more important than creative financing techniques, in terms of its preponderance in cities' budgets, is federal aid. City council and budget officers look to extralocal (i.e., federal and state) sources to enhance the size of the budget, the impact the budget can make on the direction the city takes, and the reputation and prestige of the individuals who control the revenues. The added revenue provided by federal funds allows the city and its agencies to address more needs than it could have without outside assistance. Recipient agencies of federal funds, then, are also satisfied in that they both have a larger amount of funds available to them (compared with the absence of federal funds), and can meet more "needs" as identified in their "needs assessments." Further, agency and budget officials attempt to enhance their reputations and prestige through winning larger portions of the city's capital pie while simultaneously performing their civic duty of addressing the physical plant's needs.

In effect, then, federal (or any extralocal) grant programs augment an agency's budget only by the size of the grants. But without these funds, many cities would have an inconsequential or nonexistent capital budget. For example, an official in Newark remarked that without federal grants the city's street program would be almost nonexistent. Federal funds have allowed them to undertake more projects than they could have on their own. This is not to suggest that federal grants are costless; they are not. But the costs of compliance (e.g., matching funds, master plans) are relatively minor compared with the tens of millions of federal dollars that can flow into a city's coffers (Lovell and Tobin 1981). An important point, however, is that these funds are thrown into the capital budget *after* the agency and budget officials decide on the amount of internally generated funds that will be committed to the agency. We argue that analyses of the stimulative or substitutive impact of federal grants are misguided because they ignore the capital budgetary process—a point we will discuss later.

The implication of the foregoing discussion is that the internally funded part of the capital budget (i.e., revenues that are exclusive of federal funds) will change minimally from year to year because of the built-in inertia of the bureaucratic bargaining process. The complexity of this bargaining process results in agencies relying on last year's capital budget allocation as a politically legitimate base for this year's request. Needless to say, this is slightly more complicated than the process of using last year's operating outlays as a legitimate basis for this year's operating budget request. Operating expenditures result from ongoing, day-to-day activities. Capital expenditures are project specific; once the project is completed, it needs only to be operated and maintained adequately, which is an operating cost justification, not a component of next year's capital budget request. In other words, the capital project finished last year cannot be the basis for a capital request this year. However, the aggregate of last year's capital projects does become the basis for this year's aggregate request because (1) agencies seek to achieve regular replacement cycles for capital facilities (as they wear out or become obsolete), (2) an agency's capital needs as defined by the agency are almost endless (i.e., there are more projects "on the shelves" than any agency could ever accomplish), and (3) shifts in the public's preferences and the introduction of new technology require that certain other capital projects be initiated. Hence, the total amount of an agency's request is the base for this year's request. Therefore,

Precedent is an important legitimizing device that operates at two levels in resource allocations. First, established agencies that have been previously funded have an enormous advantage over new agencies in the appropriation process. Their demands for resources at existing levels are automatically reviewed as *legitimate*. . . . Second, funding that maintains current levels of inputs has an enormous advantage over the purchase of new inputs (Larkey 1979, 99–100).

In other words, because last year's budget has been legitimized politically (by virtue of having been approved by city council), officials who seek to maintain current levels of input make ample use of the power of precedent. Of course, agency officials want to do more than maintain current levels of input; they would like to see those levels increase. However, maintaining input and output levels at least at last year's levels is affected not just by precedent but also by available revenues.

In the case of the capital budget, agency and budget officials are not as constrained by budget-balancing requirements, as they may be in the case of the operating budget. Capital budgets are virtually always unbalanced because the manner by which revenues finance the capital budget always results in a surplus. Capital budgets are financed principally from the sale of bonds, earmarked revenues, and intergovernmental grants-in-aid. The primary reason for the imbalance is unused (escrow account) bond funds. These funds are generated at a time when finance officers believe the bond market is most favorable, and when agency officials have capital projects in need of financing. Bond revenues for any city fluctuate wildly from year to year (as a quick glance at "Long-Term Debt Issues" in *City Government*

Finances attests), and capital outlays are not necessarily made immediately upon receipt of bond funds. Bond funds from a particular issuance are expended gradually, usually over several years. Ultimately, however, a city's debt is retired through taxes on the city's residents and/or user charges.

Because the debt portion of the capital budget must ultimately be retired by internally generated revenues, we argue that a balanced budget requirement, analogous to that of the operating budget, exists for the capital budget. Each year a certain amount of funds from the city must be transferred to the capital budget to retire the debt. The amount transferred can be increased in order to meet more borrowing requirements (in the event the city issues more debt) or to undertake additional projects (in a pay-as-you-go finance scheme). But the amount of the increase in city-generated revenues for the capital budget depends upon the city's capacity to generate more funds each year. As the city's revenue-generating capacity changes, part of that increase or decrease may be diverted to (or subtracted from) the capital budget. Augmenting or cutting back the capital budget, then, hinges in part on the change in own-source, or internally generated, revenues.

In addition, city officials and bureaucrats must be *willing* to dedicate a portion of the increase in city revenues to the capital budget. As internally generated revenues grow, there is not only competition among agencies for these resources at the operating level (e.g., hiring additional personnel), but also for a portion of the new resources that might find their way into the capital budget. Officials may decide not to commit any of the additional revenues to capital projects. In such situations, no increase in capital projects results because city officials are unwilling to divert a portion of the new internally generated revenues to the capital budget.

Unwillingness to augment capital outlays in such circumstances often implies a desire to expand the operating budget. City officials may pursue this course of action, even in the face of unmet capital needs, because they wish to expand city government employment. New programs can be started, other programs upgraded, and in either case new personnel hired. Diversion of more funds to the capital budget usually does not have this direct employment impact. Most local capital projects are contracted out; thus more capital outlays usually generate more private construction jobs, at least in the short-term. Expanding the city government's employment base through the operating budget results in a legitimized precedent for next year's budget request, which both enhances prestige and allows more operating needs to be addressed. Unwillingness to augment the capital budget, then, may result from how officials gauge the trade-offs between expansion of city employment rolls and a larger capital project list. Indeed, cities can (and do) decide to dedicate fewer resources to capital projects due in part to an unwillingness to pursue that course of action.

In sum, the capital budget allocates revenues to projects that are only incrementally (or decrementally) different from last year's outlays (the precedent), and capital outlays are affected by the amount of additional internally generated revenues and the officials' willingness to spend on capital projects. The amount of funds to be spent from the city's own revenues for capital projects is not affected by the receipt of federal grants. Federal funds may (indeed do) influence which projects will be funded (i.e., eligible projects) and, of course, federal funds affect the size of the total capital budget, but they do not alter significantly the incremental nature of internally generated resource allocation to the capital budget.

The Federal Variable   Although the capital budgeting theory presented above indicates that federal grants should not have a discernible effect on a city's capital outlays that are financed from its own sources, there is a large body of literature that disagrees. Many analysts take the view that federal grants substitute for own-source revenues; others conclude just the opposite — that federal grants encourage recipient governments to spend more than they otherwise would have (i.e., they are stimulative). In a review of the literature on the determinants of public spending, Inman (1979) critiques earlier approaches to identifying the determinants of local fiscal behavior. He suggests that these studies (1) have been atheoretical in that variables are incorporated which are statistically significant and produce the best goodness-of-fit statistics without any underlying conceptual framework; (2) have been erroneous in using aggregate data that combine local and state expenditures, forcing the assumption that both levels of government behave in precisely the same manner; and (3) have misspecified federal grants-in-aid — the assumption being that lump-sum and matching grants have the same impact on local and state fiscal behavior.

Gramlich and Galper (1973) address this last concern by differentiating federal grants into three types, each with a different presumed impact on fiscal behavior. Type A grants, primarily open-ended matching grants such as Medicare, Aid to Families with Dependent Children (AFDC), and Medicaid, are expected to have the greatest stimulative effect on local and state governments. That is, theoretically, governments respond by increasing their own outlays beyond what they would have spent in the absence of Type A grants. Type B, or block grants, are expected to have no appreciable effect on local/state fiscal behavior. Type C, or closed-ended categorical grants (the largest category in terms of numbers of grants), are expected to have an impact somewhere between Type A and Type B grants.

Much of the research in the last ten years has accepted this typology to some extent. Most of the recent research has relied on a demand framework devised from microeconomics. This approach requires the researcher to view the process of local fiscal choice as an "as if" preference maximization subject to a budget constraint. Preferences are specified over local public services and after tax-or-transfer incomes while the budget constraint requires local revenues from taxes and subventions to equal local expenditures on public output. The optimization process used to describe local fiscal choice yields a set of demand equations for output and local revenue (or, equivalently, private income) as a function of the net costs of outputs, before tax income, and fiscal base (Inman 1979, 274).

A series of current-period public-service demand equations and private-income (local revenue) equations based on individual preference functions are the results of this approach. The results provide price elasticities, income elasticities, and exogenous (or federal) aid elasticities. Curiously, this last output provides little consensus on an accepted elasticity value. Because of differences in how the demand models are specified, what data are used, and what unit of analysis is observed, no consistent finding emerges on the impact of federal grants (for summaries of the literature, see Inman 1979, 286–88; Broyd 1980, 23–25; Stein 1982; Advisory Commission on Intergovernmental Relations [ACIR] 1978). However, it is generally agreed that open-ended matching grants provide the greatest stimulus, closed-ended matching grants less stimulus, and nonmatching grants the least. In fact, some analysts suggest that nonmatching grants may be primarily substitutive; that is, that cities may reduce taxes or increase spending for other functions (see, inter alia, Advisory Commission on Intergovernmental Relations [ACIR] 1977; Barro 1978; Gramlich 1969).

A problem with most studies on the local response to federal aid stems from the lack of appropriate data. Scholars have had to rely on published data that are aggregated for all functions at the level of the city, county, or state. Because of this, conclusions regarding the impact of federal programs tend to suggest that many categorical grants stimulate (albeit slightly) own-source or nonfederal expenditures. At the level of total city expenditures, it may appear as if changes in federal funds correlate with changes in own-source funds. However, we would like to suggest that if a purpose of federal programs is to stimulate expenditures in the aided functional category, then the appropriate data to examine are those that are disaggregated by function. Utilization of this approach will better address the federal impact question.

We reemphasize that our view of the impact of federal aid does not square with those who see matching, categorical grants as stimulative. It is diametrically opposed. We believe that city officials generally are not induced by federal aid into spending more than they would have in the absence of federal aid. Thus, we expect that federal aid, as a variable that might affect city outlays on a particular function, will have a negligible impact.

Model Specification

The complexity of the iterative and bargaining nature of capital budgeting is almost impossible to model effectively. In one attempt to evaluate the impact of a federal program, General Revenue Sharing (GRS), on the spending patterns of five medium-sized municipalities, Larkey relies on several bureaucratic process models. However, his selection of the previous year's outlays and a revenue constraint as explanatory variables results in a distorted picture of the richness and dynamism of public budgeting. As he admits:

> The formal models assert that the broad outline of resource allocation decision processes is similar among cities. . . . The models accommodate diversity among cities in the detailed structure and content of financial decision processes by using parameters specific to functional accounts within cities, that do not correspond directly to particular decisions. Rather, these parameters . . . summarize the complex forces operating to change allocation levels (Larkey 1979, 114).

Our models imbed many of the same problems. Because they do not focus on the relevant individuals or agencies in question, they cannot be viewed as describing or explaining bureaucratic behavior. Rather, they reflect the outcomes of the interaction of "complex forces" which come together in the capital budgeting process. The primary purpose of this exercise is to compare the results of two competing models, one that conforms to our theory of the capital budgetary process as presented above, and one that contains a federal variable in order to ascertain the impact of federal grants on a city's capital spending pattern.

Capital outlays financed from sources other than federal grants can best be explained by a bureaucratic process model because decisions on capital outlays, like those on operating outlays, are made in a politicized environment. In this first model, we expect capital expenditures for a particular functional category in a given year to depend on outlays from the previous year (i.e., precedent), and year-to-year changes in own-source revenues (which reflect both the city's fiscal capacity and the city's willingness to spend a portion of any positive change on capital projects). We expect to find that the federal grants-in-aid variable will not have an impact on a city's allocation process with respect to its own, internally generated funds. Our theory of capital budgeting suggests that federal capital grants are exogenous to the process, and it is therefore appropriate for us to model only that portion of capital expenditures not financed by federal grants. Instead of focusing on total outlays or on departmental capital outlays, we model the nonfederally financed capital expenditures for each functional area. Our dependent variable in all cases is the amount of capital expenditures financed from sources other than federal grants for specific functional categories and for each individual city. The model, which we call the *Closed Model*, assumes the following form for each city:

Closed Model: $NF_{i,t}$ $= B_1 + B_2 NF_{i,t-1} + B_3 (OS_t - OS_{t-1}) + u$

where,

$NF_{i,t}$ = nonfederally financed capital outlays for function i at year t,

$NF_{i,t-1}$ = nonfederally financed capital outlays for function i at year $t-1$

$OS_t - OS_{t-1}$ = the difference in own-source revenues between year t and year $t-1$

u = normally distributed error term.

The functions for which data were collected in the site visits include street and bridges, sewer systems, and water systems (see appendix). However, insufficient data were collected for water systems, and, further, so few federal funds flowed to water systems (the amount is important for the comparative model presented below) that they are excluded from discussion in this section. Outlays for NF are in thousands of constant 1972 dollars (deflated by the city-specific Building Cost Index as calculated by the *Engineering News-Record* for streets and bridges, and deflated by the Environmental Protection Agency's (EPA) Sewer and Sewage Treatment Indexes for sewer facilities, and represent actual (not budgeted) expenditures for a specific function. NF is presented in constant-dollar terms because it represents an attempt by officials to maintain levels of output (i.e., service levels); we relax the assumption later by using current dollars in order to view the extent to which officials attempt to maintain input levels. OS in millions of constant dollars was collected from *City Government Finances* (U.S. Department of Commerce) and pertains to all internally generated revenues (except for utilities). For the three sewer treatment authorities that are not part of the city's domain, data on OS revenues were collected from U.S. Department of Commerce, Bureau of the Census, *Finances of Special Districts* for Pittsburgh (Allegheny County Sanitary Authority), from the *Annual Reports* of the Metropolitan Sewer District for Hartford, and from *Audited Financial Accounts* for the Metropolitan St. Louis Sewer District. Because NF data were not collected in comparable form for Newark's and Seattle's sewage treatment authorities, these cities are excluded from the remainder of this discussion.

There are several problems with the model. One is a data problem; the others are error terms and multicollinearity problems. As is discussed in the appendix, the number of observations per city varies from ten to twenty-one (each observation corresponds to an actual expenditure per year). The paucity of data leaves, in some cases, few degrees of freedom. However, given the problems in collecting the data, the problem of a relatively small number of observations is unavoidable.[1] Furthermore, because of the unique character of the time period for which data were collected, we expect that the explanatory power of the model will be deficient due to the fact that random shocks and unanticipated events were not modeled. The explanatory power of a model with three years of data would ordinarily be fairly strong so long as the three years represent normal times. But, from 1957 to 1977, urban and antiwar riots, creation of new programs (e.g., GRS, EPA), legal requirements (e.g., Affirmative Action), and other shocks to city governance must be expected to have had an effect on the budgetary system. Such shocks must be expected to result in lower explanatory powers than are expected of time-series budgeting studies with a small number of observations, but covering a less volatile period.

An assumption underlying this regression model is that the residuals are serially independent; that is, there is no correlation between the error term this year and the error term last year. However, where autocorrelation of the residuals was significant according to the Durbin-Watson statistic, the generalized least squares model was employed with appropriate lags. This was a problem in only a few cases and, when corrected, the statistics changed minimally. Therefore, the table presents the statistics from the ordinary least squares models only. In all such modelling, a problem in estimating the parameters may arise if there is correlation between the independent variables. If multicollinearity were to exist, step-wise regression would have been appropriate. However, this was not a problem.

Because so many studies have concluded that federal grants have had an impact on city outlays, the federal grant variable will be incorporated in a competing model. This alternative model is derived from the capital budgeting theory presented above, but now relaxes an earlier assumption, namely, that federal grants are exogenous to the capital budgeting process and therefore do not have an impact on a city's spending patterns from its own-source funds. The model that incorporates the federal grant variable assumes the following form:

Federal Model: $NF_{i,t} = B_1 + B_2NF_{i,t-1} + B_3(OS_t - OS_{t-1}) + B_4FED_{i,t} + u$
where,

$FED_{i,t}$ = federally financed capital outlays for function i at year t.

Outlays for the *FED* variable are in thousands of constant 1972 dollars (deflated like the *NF* values), and represent actual expenditures. Values for the *FED* variable in most cases were federal categorical grants (P.L. 92-500, EPA grants for sewer treatment facilities, and Federal Aid Urban Systems and other grants for city streets), but there were exceptions. Community Development Block Grants (CDBG) provided considerable revenue for street and bridge projects for Newark and Hartford after 1974, but were of minor importance for the other cities. GRS was used only by Dallas for 1975 and

Table 3.1 Regression models for street and bridge capital outlays.

City	Model	N	Intercept	NF_{t-1}	OS
Baltimore	*Closed*	10	32097.6*	−0.050	−2015.6**
			(2.151)	(−0.19)	(−2.97)
	Federal	10	42168.1*	−0.002	−2115.5**
			(−0.006)	(−0.611)	(−2.91)
Dallas	*Closed*	18	10259.9**	0.485**	20.08
			(2.374)	(2.13)	(0.42)
	Federal	18	10252.4**	0.428*	21.44
			(2.342)	(1.76)	(0.44)
Des Moines	*Closed*	17	2046.3*	0.632**	−121.33
			(1.880)	(3.27)	(−0.438)
	Federal	17	2272.6*	0.651**	−163.4
			(2.014)	(3.31)	(−0.577)
Hartford	*Closed*	18	42.9	0.7027**	18.13
			(0.388)	(2.14)	(0.955)
	Federal	18	31.1	0.464	10.86
			(0.283)	(1.22)	(0.55)
Newark	*Closed*	18	249.5**	0.303	−1.625
			(2.172)	(1.25)	(−0.23)
	Federal	18	249.5**	0.265	−0.602
			(2.101)	(0.849)	(−0.068)
New Orleans	*Closed*	10	2881.3**	0.161	353.4**
			(2.397)	(0.803)	(2.62)
	Federal	10	3527.0	0.102	388.1*
			(1.576)	(0.374)	(2.22)
Pittsburgh	*Closed*	17	3372.4*	0.301	20.45
			(2.060)	(0.963)	(0.356)
	Federal	17	4460.9**	0.121	45.03
			(2.310)	(0.341)	(0.728)
St. Louis	*Closed*	18	340.0	0.834**	−76.3
			(0.626)	(6.73)	(−1.41)
	Federal	18	405.1	0.825**	−77.5
			(0.532)	(5.618)	(−1.367)
Seattle	*Closed*	18	6909.5**	0.185	77.57
			(3.163)	(0.724)	(0.669)
	Federal	18	8238.2**	0.048	130.3
			(3.574)	(0.184)	(1.11)

Note: The selected model is italicized. The criterion for deciding which model to choose was based on the following algorithm: when "$\dfrac{(1-R^2)}{(1-k-n)^2}$ is a minimum" where k = number of regressors (Wonnacott and Wonnacott 1979, 186).

FED	F-Ratio	R^2	D.W.
—	4.44*	.559	1.28
−0.374	2.82	.585	1.34
—	2.30	.234	2.01
1.51 (0.76)	1.68	.265	2.06
—	5.37**	.433	1.42
−1.306 (−0.871)	3.77**	.465	1.41
—	2.72*	.265	1.74
0.241 (1.19)	2.33	.333	1.61
—	0.84	.101	2.03
0.033 (0.199)	0.54	.103	2.04
—	4.98**	.587	2.56
−0.16 (−0.352)	2.95	.596	2.53
—	0.69	.090	1.61
−0.88 (−1.044)	0.83	1.60	1.68
—	2.26**	.751	2.53
−0.232 (−0.126)	14.1**	.751	2.53
—	0.79	.095	1.83
−3.459 (−1.435)	1.25	.211	1.95

* = significant at <.10 level
** = significant at <.05 level
Source: Field data and published data (see text).

Table 3.2   Regression models for street and bridge
capital outlays using current dollars.

City	Model	Intercept	NF_{t-1}	OS
Dallas	*Closed*	3360.1	0.888**	40.9
		(0.919)	(4.333)	(0.981)
	Federal	5952.6	0.557*	32.5
		(1.575)	(2.021)	(0.820)
Hartford	*Closed*	−27.2	0.725**	24.1*
		(−0.260)	(3.263)	(1.825)
	Federal	−20.4	0.650*	20.6
		(0.185)	(1.880)	(1.124)

Note: Substitutions that yield the remaining equations either did not appreciably improve the explanatory power of the models (as in the street and bridge equations for Des Moines, St. Louis, Newark, Pittsburgh, and Seattle), or diminished the explanatory power (as in the street and bridge equations for Baltimore and New Orleans).

1976, but it amounted to a very small amount (less than 1 or 2 percent of total street capital outlays). Therefore, the impact of the *FED* variable on street and sewer capital outlays refers principally to categorical grants. If the Closed Model reasonably estimates capital expenditures for function *i* that are not financed by federal grants, and if federal grants do not influence capital outlays as we suggest, then it should have less bias and variance in its estimating form than the Federal Model. The rule adopted for model selection is based on the following: "If the data determines the order that the regressors are being included, add regressors [k] until $(1-R^2)/(1-k-n)^2$ is a minimum" (Wonnacott and Wonnacott 1979, 186).

Empirical Results

Using the selection rule, all nine equations for street capital outlays are better modeled with the Closed than Federal Model, and five of the seven equations for sewer capital expenditures are better modeled with the Closed Model. (The selected models are italicized.) Table 3.1 presents the statistics for street capital outlays. Of the nine equations, only four have significant *F*-ratios and acceptable coefficients of determination. For two, Des Moines and Seattle, the coefficient for the precedent variable (i.e., NF_{t-1}) is statistically significant; for the other two, Baltimore and New Orleans, the differencing of the own-source revenue variable is significant. For the other cities, the explanatory power of the model is quite low. However, it should be emphasized that the purpose of the exercise is less one of estimating coefficients than evaluating whether the addition of a federal variable appreciably improves the models. It seems that, as far as

FED	F-Ratio	R^2	D.W.
—	10.51**	.584	2.22
3.794 (1.687)	8.82**	.654	2.22
—	5.39**	.418	1.49
0.067 (0.292)	3.40**	.422	1.45

* = significant at <.10 level
** = significant at <.05 level
Source: Field data and published data (see text).

the street and bridge capital outlays equations are concerned, the federal impact is not significant.

If we relax the assumption that asserts that agencies and officials attempt to maintain service level outputs, another set of results emerge. By specifying the NF and FED variables as current-dollar expenditures (rather than constant dollar)—which assumes officials and agencies try to maintain their input levels (i.e., the amount of resources they receive)—two additional cities have acceptable F-ratios and coefficients of determination for the Closed Model. Dallas's coefficient of determination increases to .58 and Hartford's to .42. In both cases the coefficient for the lagged NF variable is statistically significant (and for Hartford the OS coefficient is significant) and the F-ratio is statistically significant (table 3.2). Again, when current and constant dollars are considered, six of the cities' own-source financed capital expenditure patterns are better modeled with the Closed Model than the Federal Model. The coefficients of determination for the remaining three are quite low, less than .25. Further, none is better estimated with the Federal Model.

Preference for the Closed Model over the Federal Model is less certain for sewer capital outlays. Although all but two of the cities' sewer capital outlays are better modeled with the Closed Model, three have F-ratios and coefficients of determination that would be considered acceptable (see table 3.3). Of these three, two are Closed Models, Hartford and Dallas, with a statistically significant coefficient for the lagged variable. One is a Federal Model, Pittsburgh, with all three coefficients statistically significant. Only one notable shift takes place when NF and FED are reported as current dollars. Baltimore's equation becomes significant for the Federal

Table 3.3 Regression models for sewer system capital outlays

City	Model	N	Intercept	NF_{t-1}	OS
Baltimore	Closed	10	3805.2	0.346	−21.94
			(1.760)	(1.01)	(−0.342)
	Federal	10	3799.2*	0.155	0.521
			(1.832)	(0.429)	(0.008)
Dallas	*Closed*	18	3491.6**	0.530**	9.851
			(2.692)	(2.989)	(0.917)
	Federal	18	3405.2**	0.555**	9.228
			(2.547)	(2.966)	(0.835)
Des Moines	*Closed*	17	1157.7**	0.140	143.4
			(2.523)	(0.544)	(1.14)
	Federal	17	1092.5*	0.151	140.6
			(2.106)	(0.563)	(1.08)
Hartford	*Closed*	9	201.9	0.843**	−1111.7
			(0.09)	(2.72)	(−0.938)
	Federal	9	223.6	0.797*	−1174.3
			(0.091)	(1.936)	(−0.882)
New Orleans	*Closed*	10	2376.1	0.203	2.476
			(1.756)	(0.544)	(0.018)
	Federal	10	2974.6*	0.128	82.89
			(1.973)	(0.332)	(0.503)
Pittsburgh	Closed	14	968.6	0.596**	−337.3
			(1.15)	(2.530)	(−0.192)
	Federal	14	901.4**	−0.174**	−768.6**
			(5.968)	(−2.911)	(−2.42)
St. Louis	*Closed*	20	5710.8	0.207	−1019.1
			(1.651)	(0.84)	(−0.519)
	Federal	20	5899.4	0.230	−944.8
			(1.643)	(0.872)	(−0.492)

Note: The selected model is italicized. The criterion for deciding which model to choose was based on the following algorithm: when "$\dfrac{(1-R^2)}{(1-k-n)^2}$ is a minimum" where k = number of regressors (Wonnacott and Wonnacott 1979, 186).

Model and the coefficient for the federal variable becomes statistically significant (table 3.4). (Another change is that the coefficient of determination for Dallas improves to .79.) For the remaining three equations, the explanatory power of either model is poor (less than .25). Thus, for sewer capital outlays, the comparison between the two models results in a less than obvious situation: two of the seven cities are better estimated with

FED	F-Ratio	R^2	D.W.
—	0.51	.128	1.95
−0.221 (1.267)	0.91	.312	1.77
—	4.48**	.373	1.65
−0.081 (−0.557)	2.95*	.387	1.69
—	0.85	.108	1.62
0.192 (0.311)	0.56	.114	1.62
—	3.96*	.569	2.54
0.074 (0.197)	2.23	.572	2.41
—	0.15	.042	1.91
−0.121 (−0.936)	0.39	.164	2.22
—	3.25*	.371	1.32
0.814** (18.19)	177.35**	.982	2.29
—	0.71	.077	2.01
−0.106 (−0.312)	0.48	.083	1.88

Data for Newark and Seattle were not collected in comparable form; hence they are excluded from this table.
* = significant at <.10 level
** = significant at <.05 level
Source: Field data and published data (see text).

the Closed Model and two with the Federal Model.

We suggest that one reason for the differences between the two series of equations (street and sewer capital outlays) and the influence of the selected variables is in the manner in which the different capital facilities are financed. Sewer systems are funded almost exclusively from revenue bonds (amortized by user charges) and/or user charges with a sprinkling of prop-

Table 3.4   Regression models for sewer system
capital outlays using current dollars.

City	Model	Intercept	NF_{t-1}	OS
Baltimore	Closed	4558.9*	0.534	−68.4
		(1.898)	(1.694)	(−0.781)
	Federal	4301.1*	0.154	−27.9
		(2.131)	(0.471)	(−0.366)
Dallas	*Closed*	1137.4	0.875**	14.5*
		(1.388)	(7.278)	(1.912)
	Federal	1240.8	0.853**	14.3*
		(1.201)	(4.851)	(1.817)

Note: Substitutions which yield the remaining equations either did not appreciably improve the explanatory power of the models (as in the sewer equations for Des Moines, New Orleans, Pittsburgh, and St. Louis), or diminished the explanatory power (as in the sewer equations for Hartford).

erty taxes. Capital outlays for street systems are financed primarily from general obligation bonds (amortized principally by tax revenues) with some help in some cases from motor vehicle fuel tax revenues returned to cities from states (the collection agents). Thus, streets, as a functional category, competes with other infrastructural categories and, therefore, tends to receive only incremental amounts of capital funds. This is consistent with our theory, and is demonstrated by the results of six of the nine equations. Sewer systems, on the other hand, do not fit as neatly into our theory of capital budgeting because of their quasi-autonomous nature. That is, sewer departments and authorities may be better able to escape an incremental budgeting pattern and focus more directly on physical needs than other infrastructural categories funded through a capital budget. Needs is a variable that was not incorporated in the model due to the problem of operationalizing it over time. Raising sewer and water rates to meet system needs is perceived as less politically volatile than raising tax rates, which may be necessary to meet street and bridge needs. This is supported by Meltsner (1971), who reports that reaction to tax increase recommendations were intensely negative in Oakland, though a proposal for an increase in the sewer service charge was, by comparison, a nonissue. The difference may be, as a recent study reports, that user charges are viewed as equitable in that the consumer pays for what he uses (Cline and Shannon 1982). The political volatility of user charges is less than that of general taxes (property, income, sales).

This may also help to explain the disparate physical conditions of the infrastructure categories in chapter 1. To the extent that the condition index approximates the adequacy and performance of the selected infrastructure

FED	F-Ratio	R^2	D.W.
—	1.47	.296	1.84
0.284* (1.990)	2.72	.576	1.51
—	28.6**	.783	1.81
0.025 (0.175)	17.9**	.793	1.80

* = significant at <.10 level.
** = significant at <.05 level.
Source: Field data and published data (see text).

categories, the street and bridge systems are generally in poorer condition than the water and sewer systems. In part, then, their physical condition may be due to the political volatility of the funding mechanism: user charges are seen as equitable, technical, and nonpoliticizable, which allows sewer and water authorities to better address their capital needs; taxes are more politicizable, which restricts street departments from meeting their capital needs.

This relative insulation from political vagaries, then, may allow waste-water treatment authorities to be influenced by federal grants. In other words, these authorities not only maintain their capital replacement or improvement plans but they also augment own-source financed capital expenditures more than they would without the federal grants. This is, at least, a plausible explanation. Two of the four statistically significant cases might be regarded in such a manner (Baltimore, a city department at the time of data collection, and Pittsburgh, an authority). The extent to which other sewer authorities and departments fit the above explanation or the theory of capital budgeting as outlined earlier is questionable. It does appear, however, that the models as specified for street and bridge capital outlays tend to support the capital budgeting theory that suggests that the process is incremental and that the impact of federal grants on capital outlays financed from the city's revenue base is not a significant factor.

Federal Aid Biases

Federal grants are not without effect, however. Biases do exist and the cumulative effect of many years of financing local infrastructure has created problems. We now turn to a discussion of those impacts.

Maintenance and Matching Requirements   Most federal categorical programs designed for cities' infrastructural activities formally exclude the use of funds for maintenance activities. For example, federal highway programs supply funds only for capital purposes. This aid was exclusively for capital expenditures until 1976. And although the Federal-Aid Highway Acts of 1976 and 1978 authorized some funds for "resurfacing, rehabilitation and restoration" (the "3Rs") of highways and bridges, the amount was minuscule ($175 million in 1976, and $275 million provided by the 1978 Act for 1981) compared to the cost estimates of restoring the system (approximately $20 billion) (Whitman 1979, 37–38). Because of the lack of maintenance funds, states and localities may be encouraged to defer maintenance of the roadway until it needs to be restored. The 1982 Surface Transportation Assistance Act increased funds for highway purposes by raising the tax rate per gallon of fuel by five cents. The act also raised the funds for "4R" activities (reconstruction was added) to 40 percent of total federal highway funds. Although the repair needs of the states' highway systems will be better addressed, a bias against traditional maintenance activities still exists in the design of the federal aid highway program (Pagano forthcoming). As one report suggests:

The way that Federal grant programs were designed has discouraged state and local officials from developing effective maintenance procedures. . . . The bias in favor of new construction runs across all Federal programs. In a survey of state and local governments . . . 90 percent of the respondents indicated that Federal capital funds cause them to lower the priorities they attach to maintenance and repair. . . . Some states deliberately allow their roads to deteriorate until they reach a point where Federal funds would be available for "major rehabilitation" (Lehman Brothers 1984, 8).

Sewage treatment authorities may also be encouraged to construct or reconstruct treatment facilities because: (1) the law (P.L. 92-500) requires that certain standards be met; and (2) the cost-sharing program under which the federal government until 1984 subsidized 75 percent of capital costs (since 1984 reduced to 55 percent) seldom overburdens the authorities. However, the fact that there is no provision for maintenance and operation of the facilities (maintenance is a 100-percent local responsibility) is cause for some concern. Because the law is relatively recent, the facilities built under P.L. 92-500 are new and not in dire need of maintenance. No one is certain that the treatment authorities will maintain, or have the incentive to maintain, their facilities adequately (Whitman 1979). This is not to suggest that conditions will worsen. Indeed, replacement of old facilities is beneficial. We suggest only that maintenance of the new facilities may not be adequate.

Furthermore, many categorical grants that are wholly financed by the federal and/or state governments with no local participation may nevertheless be rejected on the basis of the project's future maintenance needs. Because these categorical grants formally exclude maintenance, the burden of maintaining the facility falls squarely on the shoulders of the local government. The inability or unwillingness to increase local revenues, therefore, may mean that the local government refuses millions of dollars for capital outlays. The city of Hartford, for example, initially declined several million dollars in federal and state funds for construction of a Skywalk that would have linked many of the downtown business buildings. The reason for rejecting this aid, according to the city manager and the assistant city manager, was that the city would have had to maintain the structure, which would require higher taxes. According to the finance director, the project was finally approved, but only after the owners of the buildings that Skywalk was to connect agreed to assume the maintenance costs. Indeed, many cities can hardly afford to continue their present maintenance programs, let alone take on new maintenance responsibilities.

Fear of future maintenance costs is not the only reason for rejecting federal and state monies. Many categorical programs require that localities share the cost of construction. For some cities, the matching requirement can be prohibitive. For example, New Orleans's capital budget for fiscal years 1979–83 (City of New Orleans 1978) contained very few projects other than those that were federally financed, and the director of streets suggested that federally financed projects that require a local match, such as the Federal Aid Urban Systems program, might never begin because New Orleans might not have funds even for matching purposes. Thus, in addition to the difficulty of generating sufficient revenues for maintenance purposes, many cities also are strained to generate sufficient revenues for the matching requirements of categorical grants.

This is not to suggest that categorical programs are never timely or helpful to urban areas. In fact, in growing areas, federal programs often correspond to city needs. Growing urban areas need infrastructure. Because there is a demand for new construction of public facilities in growing areas, the availability of federal capital grants often directly corresponds to the needs of growing cities. On the other hand, older cities, already victims of shrinking revenue bases, are less able to take advantage of infrastructural grants because of the procapital, antimaintenance orientation of such grants. Federal capital programs of the categorical type, then, may be differentially advantageous to some (i.e., newer, growing) cities.

In the past decade, of course, block grants, General Revenue Sharing (GRS) and emergency relief (antirecessionary) programs have attempted to complement categorical programs with unrestricted funds. For example, it has been estimated that 30 to 40 percent of revenue sharing monies have been used for financing capital expenditures with no strings attached (Nathan, Manvel, Calkins, et al. 1975; Nathan et al. 1977). Certainly the largest federal program, GRS, cannot be criticized for not addressing cities' maintenance needs. GRS is an all-purpose program, and GRS funds, if transferred to a city's General Fund (which finances operating expenses of the city), are not directly traceable. Thus, it is not clear how much of GRS is expended on maintenance programs, and how much on administrative, clerical, and staff salaries. In addition, GRS funds are often accounted for in only one department—often in the police or fire department—which releases revenue to other departments. GRS funds, then, are not expended directly by, say, the street department for maintenance activities, although as part of the city's General Fund, they indirectly contribute to maintenance.

Because of the fungibility of GRS funds, it is difficult to attribute any direct impact on maintenance outlays, but if GRS were distributed to all activities proportionally, maintenance would, we presume, not suffer. In fact, however, for street and bridge maintenance outlays, it appears from table 3.5 that the years prior to the introduction of GRS proved to be more beneficial to maintenance activities than the period after its adoption. Note in particular the dramatic decline in current-dollar street maintenance expenditures for Newark between 1968 and 1977, as well as between 1974 and 1977, even though the city expended 123.8 percent more in FY 1977 than in FY 1968. In all cities except Pittsburgh, total city expenditures more than doubled in this ten-year period, while current-dollar street and bridge maintenance outlays increased minimally. After receipt of GRS funds in FY 1973 (or 1974), one might expect street and bridge maintenance activities to benefit to some degree. That appears not to have happened, except for two cases (Pittsburgh and Seattle), and the only reason Pittsburgh appears to be a deviant case is that during the last two years of the study period, outlays rose by 21 percent. Seattle is an exception because of very low outlays in 1974; if 1973 or 1975 were used as the base year, the increase would be minuscule.

Hence, although GRS is not inherently biased against maintenance activities, cities appear not to have spent their increased funds on street maintenance despite the fact that the condition table in chapter 1 indicates the need for such maintenance. Larkey suggests one plausible explanation:

The degree of "fiscal pressure" on recipient units of government is the single most important determinant of how GRS funds affect recipients' fiscal behavior. . . . When fiscal pressure exists, GRS funds tend to be merged with the other general operating funds and used to support recurrent expenditure obligations (e.g., existing personnel commitments). When "fiscal pressure" does not exist, GRS funds will be used for: (1) revenue displacement; (2) the accumulation of surplus; (3)

Table 3.5 Total city expenditures vs. maintenance expenditures
for streets and bridges.

	Change in City Expenditures 1968–77	Change in City Expenditures 1974–77	Change in Maintenance Expenditures			
			Streets		Bridges	
			1968–77	1974–77	1968–77	1974–77
Baltimore	+ 163.0%	+ 38.7%	− 0.2%[1]	− 5.1%	+ 3.1%	+ 5.6%
Dallas	+ 144.2	+ 14.2	+ 8.1	+ 1.9	NA	0.0
Des Moines	+ 126.3	+ 47.3	+ 75.1	+ 21.1[2]	+ 63.2	+ 41.2
Hartford	+ 198.1	+ 14.0	+ 49.3	0.0	NA	NA
New Orleans	+ 113.9	+ 35.1	+ 54.9	+ 13.5	NA	0.0
Newark	+ 123.8	+ 17.3	− 34.5	− 22.5	0.0	0.0
Pittsburgh	+ 90.0	+ 27.6	+ 162.7	+ 39.9	NA	NA
St. Louis	+ 120.2	+ 28.9	+ 82.8	− 16.2	NA	NA
Seattle	+ 107.6	+ 26.8	+ 86.9	+ 45.0	+ 47.1	− 0.6

1. FY 1971–1977.
2. Estimated.
Source: For columns 1 and 2, U.S. Department of Commerce, Bureau of the Census, *City Government Finances;* for columns 3, 4, 5, and 6, field data.

increased funding of basic services; and/or (4) capital projects and other nonrecurrent expenditure obligations (Larkey 1979, 218).

It appears that the antimaintenance orientation, as well as the inability of many federal programs to understand the differential capabilities of cities to raise the local match, do indeed imply that biases inhere in the design of many categorical federal grants.

Project Selection In our theory of capital budgeting, we suggested that federal grants do not influence decisions by local officials to augment capital outlays that are funded from internal sources. We stated, in fact, that federal grants are exogenous to the capital budgeting process. This should not be misconstrued to mean that federal grants have no impact. Rather, we do not expect cities to increase their own commitment to capital projects in response to federal grant availability. However, the selection of a given project from the list of needs will often be affected by the possibility of the receipt of federal grants.

For example, federal wastewater treatment grants can only be expended for eligible activities. The Environmental Protection Agency (EPA) estimates a nationwide backlog of over $93 billion for Category VI needs (Treatment and/or Control of Stormwater), which is an activity ineligible for federal water pollution control grants. In addition, after 1 October

1984, Categories IIIB (Replacement and/or Rehabilitation), IVA (New Collector Systems), and V (Combined Sewer Overflows) became ineligible for funding, with 1982 backlog needs estimated at $55 billion (U.S. EPA 1982). (Such EPA needs estimates estimate the costs of treatment that will be necessary to comply with effluent standards of the Clean Water Act.) It has been argued that local authorities have been induced into shifting their own capital funds from their regular replacement activities to federal grant eligible activities. If this is true, the wastewater treatment authority may spend the same amount of its own funds for capital purposes as it would have in the absence of the federal grant, but it spends these funds on the matching portion of an EPA eligible activity. In fact, the insignificant FED variables for some cities in table 3.3 can be interpreted as evidence that wastewater treatment authorities or departments have shifted their capital projects toward eligible federal programs and away from their normal capital (replacement) programs. In other words, if wastewater treatment authorities are not altering their own total capital spending, the fact that they must pay 25 percent of the total cost of federal aid eligible projects must mean that they are spending less on nonmatching, local responsibility capital projects. Once the sewage treatment facility has been upgraded, internally generated funds will probably be shifted back to these normal capital projects. But federal wastewater treatment grants strongly influence which projects are currently targeted for inclusion in capital improvement plans.

The current design of federal highway grants may be having a similar effect. For example, New Orleans's five-year capital plan for 1979–83 contained only highway projects in which the Federal Highway Trust Fund participated. City-owned streets, a 100 percent local responsibility, were not included. In part, this was due to the fact that projected revenues for the local match (from bond sales) would probably be forthcoming only if they would be used to leverage federal dollars—that is, to get the "biggest bang for the buck." Officials in Newark indicated that without federal programs, Newark's street program would be practically nonexistent. Projects eligible for federal aid tend to be placed at the top of the list of funded projects even if other, noneligible projects seem to represent a greater need. As city officials told us in most of the cities: Why forego extra dollars of federal aid when the alternative is to do less—even if it means not addressing our highest priority needs. At least something is getting done!

Again, the point is that federal grants do affect the decision-making process. Eligibility for federal funding often enhances a project's priority on a city's needs list. This may mean that eligible projects supplant projects that otherwise represent greatest need. Thus, federal grants do indeed bias the process of project selection.

Table 3.6   Federal intergovernmental expenditures specifically for capital outlay purposes, by function, 1957 to 1976–77 (current dollars).

Period (Fiscal Years)	Total[1]	High-ways	Housing and Urban Renewal[2]	Health and Hospitals	Sewerage	Airports	Education	Mass Trans-portation
1957	1,172	944	112	30	1	19	66	—
1958	1,777	1,477	125	45	17	42	71	—
1959	2,969	2,580	182	51	36	56	64	—
1960	3,353	2,906	223	58	40	56	70	—
1961	3,093	2,586	275	66	44	63	59	—
1962	3,257	2,748	309	60	42	57	41	—
1963	3,533	2,951	359	64	51	52	53	—
1963–1964	4,453	3,615	543	115	66	65	39	—
1964–1965	5,035	3,983	675	161	75	71	29	—
1965–1966	4,870	3,953	607	120	81	54	50	5
1966–1967	5,045	4,059	670	116	83	61	44	12
1967–1968	5,590	4,291	787	152	118	74	133	35
1968–1969	5,991	4,352	921	161	135	102	178	142
1969–1970	6,944	4,608	1,609	162	175	82	190	118
1970–1971	7,603	4,987	1,611	93	475	70	179	188
1971–1972	8,120	5,108	1,981	42	411	119	200[3]	259
1972–1973	9,936	5,276	2,121	152	681	231	1,200[3]	275
1973–1974	9,671	4,555	2,391	148	1,806	253	—	518
1974–1975	10,976	4,754	2,734	88	2,234	305	—	861
1975–1976	13,764	6,243	2,820	182	2,803	294	—	1,422
1976–1977	15,411	6,173	2,914	NA	4,052	381	—	1,891

1. These are estimated totals.
2. Housing payments included here do not specifically finance construction but subsidize low-rent housing undertaken by local governments, and thus indirectly foster capital outlays for public housing. This is noted by Manvel 1965, 60. The actual capital component is quite small. Estimates are available for 1967–1974 from *Special Analysis* P and Q of the *Budget of the United States*. Figures for those years in millions respectively are 7, 49, 91, 132, 143, 157, 183, and 136.
3. Schneiderman (1975).
Source: Data through 1965 from Manvel (1965), 1966–1977 from U.S. Department of Commerce, *Government Finances*, tables 6, 7, and 10 in various years.

City Reliance on Federal Grants

Besides their impact on project selection, federal grants also have a tremendous impact on the size of the total capital budget and, ultimately, on the quality of a city's infrastructure or capital plant. Federal and state

Table 3.7 Nonlocal aid as a percentage of general
city revenue (excluding utility revenues).

	Federal Aid as a Percentage of General Revenues			
	FY 1967–68	FY 1972–73	FY 1976–77	FY 1980–81
Baltimore	2.4%	12.4%	15.9%	18.5%
Dallas	7.5	4.4	13.3	13.2
Des Moines	2.6	13.6	10.5	10.6
Hartford	0.2	9.5	21.6	15.2
New Orleans	2.3	19.5	26.0	26.7
Newark	0.9	4.9	12.7	5.4
Pittsburgh	7.7	19.6	24.6	25.8
St. Louis	1.8	17.3	19.5	—
Seattle	1.2	19.8	21.3	15.3

capital grants have enabled cities to provide safer drinking water, better and smoother riding surfaces for motor vehicles, sewer systems with advanced or secondary treatment, more efficient and effective transportation systems, etc. The federal government's participation in providing state and local infrastructure has not been inconsequential. Table 3.6 illustrates the growth of federal capital involvement with seven major categories of spending. As federal (and state) involvement has grown, the proportion of federal aid (and intergovernmental aid, which includes state) has increased at a faster rate than have cities' internally generated funds. As table 3.7 indicates, extralocal aid as a percentage of each city's general revenues has increased markedly since the mid-1960s.

More important to our purposes, federal grants to the two selected infrastructural categories (the third, water, receives almost no federal aid and is therefore excluded) are comparatively large, considering each city's total capital outlays for sewer systems and streets and bridges (table 3.8). Two observations are in order. First, federal aid is a greater proportion of total capital outlays by function for those cities identified in chapter 2 as relatively fiscally stressed. Second, federal aid is a fairly small proportion of the fiscally healthy cities' capital outlays. (The glaring exception is Baltimore's capital outlays for streets. But the reason for the high proportion of federal aid in this case is the fact that, unlike the other cities, Baltimore receives federal interstate highway funds). This does not imply that cities are investing less, but rather that federal capital grants are grow-

Intergovernmental Aid as a Percentage of General Revenues			
FY 1967–68	FY 1972–73	FY 1976–77	FY 1980–81
50.7%	61.2%	65.0%	63.1%
10.0	8.2	15.8	15.1
14.8	29.4	34.3	29.2
35.9	30.2	43.8	46.6
16.9	33.5	39.9	37.8
23.7	51.3	60.3	69.9
16.2	30.8	41.6	39.2
8.6	26.7	28.9	—
19.9	37.2	35.4	33.6

Source: Derived from U.S. Department of Commerce, Bureau of The Census, *City Government Finances*, various years.

ing at a much faster rate than the growth in internally financed capital outlays. Further, the total amount of federal grants for the fiscally stressed cities, by the late 1970s, had become an alarming proportion of total capital outlays.

This point is illustrated by capital outlays for sewers. The cities in this survey all received federal wastewater treatment grants. Wastewater treatment grants require a 25 percent local match (which increased to 45 percent 1 October 1984). We would expect that those sewage treatment authorities that maintained their pregrant capital outlay levels would have a lower reliance on federal grants (as illustrated by the proportions in table 3.6) than those authorities that reduced their pregrant capital outlay levels. Thus, the higher proportion of reliance on federal contributions for the fiscally stressed cities indicates that those cities may be reducing their own-source capital outlays. In five, ten, or twenty years, when these treatment facilities begin to deteriorate and are in need of reconstruction, a crisis may arise if these cities do not maintain their levels of own-source capital outlay.

In the cases of both sewage treatment facilities and streets and bridges, the total amount of capital outlays would have been significantly less without federal aid than it was with federal participation. As a result, the size and quality of the public capital plant is now larger than it would have been. Thus, another consequence of federal grants is that cities have larger and higher quality infrastructure systems (i.e., higher engineering standards)

Table 3.8   Federal contributions as a percentage of capital outlays.

Central Cities (least fiscal stress to most fiscal stress)	Streets and Bridges		Sewer System	
	1957–77	1968–77	1957–77	1968–77
Dallas	3.4%	7.8%	21.3%	29.0%
Des Moines	4.0	6.5	24.1	34.8
Seattle	1.7	2.7	NA	NA
Pittsburgh	8.1	11.2	NA	50.0
Baltimore	NA	69.1	NA	51.2
St. Louis	3.1	24.6	36.9	28.5
New Orleans	NA	31.5	NA	56.7
Hartford	60.5	63.3	NA	34.5
Newark	49.8	56.7	NA	NA

NA = not available, or not available in comparable form.
Source: Field data.

to manage and maintain than they probably would have otherwise.

As unremarkable as that may sound, it does present increasing problems to cities that experience declining revenue bases, outmigration, and economic growth problems. There is seldom federal aid for maintenance activities, and cities are now required to maintain and operate capital plants that are larger and of higher quality than they would have built on their own. Fiscally stressed cities, in part because of the large size of their infrastructures, are finding their operations and maintenance responsibility increasingly difficult to perform adequately (e.g., witness the physical condition of streets and bridges for the fiscally stressed cities in table 1.2). And even growing cities will reach the point when they will need to make significant repairs. Whether these needs will be met is a moot point. The fact is that the federal grants have made a difference. Thus, because of the influence of federal grants, cities have to operate and maintain larger or higher quality infrastructure systems than they would have in the absence of federal grant programs.

Summary and Policy Implications

We contend that the outputs of the capital budgeting process mirror those of the operating budget as far as the incremental allocation of internally generated revenues for capital purposes is concerned. We argue that for capital budget activities that rely on tax revenues from the General Fund, an incremental process adequately explains the patterns of outlays. The impact of federal grants is minimal in terms of altering the total amount of funds a locality is willing to invest from its own sources. For activities that rely on user charges and are isolated from competition with other activities, the incremental model may only be partially accurate. These functions may allocate resources more on the basis of need or physical condition of the facility. However, federal grants may induce such facilities to spend more on capital projects from internally generated funds than they otherwise would have. In both cases, federal grants obviously increase the physical size and quality of a city's infrastructure, which necessitates larger operating and maintenance outlays. However, the grants do not usually fund maintenance activities, which, especially for the older cities, have registered the largest growth in needs.

Budget and agency officials are caught in a bind. On the one hand, they want to increase outlays (in order to address needs and to augment their own prestige); on the other, a strong incremental force is at work that acts to hold down needed increases in capital maintenance outlays. To compound the problem, the size of the infrastructure system is growing very rapidly, and outlays are rising very slowly, leaving an increasingly large gap between system needs and revenues. This gap can be partially bridged if officials sense their electorate's willingness to channel revenues to capital facilities. Willingness to spend, within the constraints of the city's capacity to generate additional funds, has increased in the past few years as media coverage of the deteriorating infrastructure and the news sensations of collapsed bridges (e.g., I-95 in 1983) and water breaks (e.g., Paterson in 1983) apparently affect the preferences of citizens for, minimally, a safe infrastructure. We explore the recent improvement in the public's receptiveness to capital expenditures in the next chapter.

Willingness to address infrastructure needs and the generation of sufficient revenues are factors over which the cities themselves have control (except to the extent that national or regional economic problems affect cities' fiscal bases). The cities have considerably less control over the panoply of federal grant offerings. Cities must decide how to respond to the offer of federal aid, and that response is conditioned by the design of the grants. Current indications are that state and local governments are channeling a larger and larger portion of their revenues to projects that have a federal match. This is because of the design of federal grants which encourages states and localities to get the "biggest bang for the buck" (see Pagano forthcoming). This action necessarily reduces funds for maintenance activities (by transferring internally generated revenues to the capital budget for matching purposes), and it encourages the selection of federal-aid eligible projects over city-determined needed projects. Although more needs may be addressed through this action, the situation is improved only in a perverse sense. State and local governments view maximizing capital program work loads without significantly increasing own-source financial contributions as an improvement. But maintaining existing infrastructural systems rather than expanding or completely replacing them would cost all levels of government less. Cities that are not experiencing increases in infrastructure use should therefore be encouraged to maintain what they have. The present design of most federal grants allows only capital projects to be considered as eligible for federal funds. Even the one exception, the 4R provisions of the federal-aid highway program (resurfacing, restoration, rehabilitation, and reconstruction), does not allow maintenance as an eligible activity. It is true that resurfacing (usually considered to be maintenance) has been eligible since 1976, but other traditional highway maintenance activities (e.g., pothole filling, slurry seals, etc.) are still ineligible.

Times are changing. Ten or twenty years ago, many communities and states had inadequate and very poor public capital facilities. Federal grants aided the provision of capital facilities to a larger and larger segment of the population. Those facilities must now be maintained. The design of federal grants does not generally provide the autonomy to local governments to decide how and where funds should be spent. Eligible activities do not include maintenance of capital facilities. Activities, such as maintenance, that are not eligible for a federal match may be supplanted by activities that are eligible, even if the noneligible activities appear high on a priority list or a needs assessment. Federal policy for the 1980s and 1990s must be keenly aware of the true needs of localities. Allowing local governments to decide where funds need to be spent would go a long way in beginning to address the deteriorating infrastructure problem.

4. Competing City Needs
Social vs. Physical

Our focus to this point has been on cities' developmental or economic overhead capital (EOC) activities, as identified in the first chapter. Among these activities, our major focus has been on providing infrastructure. For the most part, the physical condition of the infrastructure in the cities we have examined has indeed deteriorated. This phenomenon is not fully explained by the fiscal stress of cities. Neither is it explained by the involvement of extralocal governments. Although federal funding, which is usually biased against maintaining facilities, has certainly provided funds for infrastructure which would not otherwise have been forthcoming, cities are not spending any more of their own-source revenues than they would have spent in the absence of federal grants.

In this chapter we broaden the scope of our analysis to include social overhead capital (SOC), or redistributive and allocational, activities of cities. The purpose of this chapter is twofold: first, we briefly discuss the SOC dimension and the budgetary trade-offs between SOC and EOC activities in a world of finite resources. In this context, the first part of this chapter is a historical examination of the competition between SOC and EOC activities within city budgets. Our purpose is to ascertain whether there has been dominance of either social (SOC) or developmental (EOC) goals as reflected in budgetary behavior in cities over the past twenty to twenty-five years. Second, we refine the conceptual framework of our study, which relies on separating city expenditures according to two broad purposes—either they serve a developmental (primarily economic) function, or they serve a redistributional or non-developmental (primarily social) function. Refinement is necessary because our knowledge about whether the public sector stimulates economic growth through public investments or, conversely, whether the public sector responds to prior private investment decisions are clearly in an inchoate stage. Before addressing this latter problem—a problem inherent in much of the urban policy literature—we examine the competing need of SOC and EOC activities in order to ascertain whether cities have been oriented toward social (SOC) or developmental (EOC) needs in the past twenty to twenty-five years.

Budgetary Trade-offs

We suggested earlier that one reason for the infrastructure dilemma has been the inability of cities to generate sufficient revenues. Here we take this argument one step farther, and look to the competition for scarce resources between infrastructural and social concerns as a possible determinant of levels of infrastructural investment. There has been a built-in assumption to the fiscal stress argument that if revenues were available or if the revenue base were stronger, cities would increase maintenance and capital outlays. Obviously, available revenue is a necessary condition for investment, but not a sufficient condition. Public and/or official willingness to make such expenditures must also be present.

Willingness to commit scarce resources was a theme of a conference on maintaining and designing urban infrastructures sponsored by the National Research Council (Hanson 1984). During the conference, one official of a large investment firm suggested that underinvestment in public infrastructure during the past ten to twenty years could be attributed to official response to taxpayer indifference or hostility toward increasing the tax rate. Taxpayer resistance to increasing the tax rate has resulted in official decisions to defer or ignore needed expansion and repair. Entrenched interests within cities' bureaucratic structures have made it impossible for cities to shift priorities from already-funded city functions to providing and maintaining the infrastructure (as Wildavsky's argument on incrementalism suggests [1964]). Public capital investment has fallen as a result. Indeed, the U.S. General Accounting Office reported that public capital investment as a percentage of the gross national product (GNP) has fallen fairly steadily since 1968 (see figure 4.1). According to one view, the decline should be attributed at least partly to the fact that the political system is responsive to citizen needs and demands (Tiebout 1956). The budget is the battlefield upon which competing interests and values struggle for favors. Expenditure patterns can be attributed to the results of this competition among relevant groups and individuals. Therefore, if there is inadequate pressure for public capital investment, then that failure will be reflected in declining expenditures.

Hartford's city manager expressed his concern about declining infrastructural investments, but added that he and city council had been under enormous pressure for years to increase delivery of social services. The political pressure, he maintained, could not be (indeed, was not) ignored. Supporters for infrastructure are few and far between. At the National Research Council's symposium, Oakland's city manager recommended

Figure 4.1   State and Local Capital Investment as a Percentage of
Gross National Product.

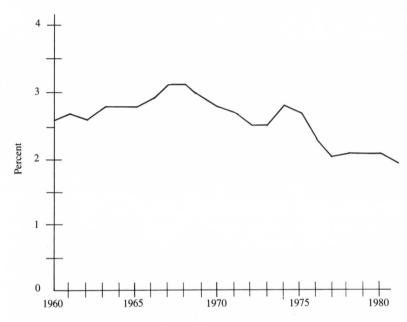

Source: U.S. General Accounting Office (1982, 15).

wryly that one way of counterbalancing the political pressure would be to
organize a Friends of the Sewers group! Although he drew sympathetic
chuckles from the crowd, his point was more than tongue-in-cheek. It was
an acknowledgment that decision makers are influenced by political pressure and that groups pressing for social services cannot easily be shunned,
despite graphic demonstrations of the alarming condition and needs of the
infrastructure. Such counterbalancing pressure groups have, in fact, been
adopted in some cities. New York, for example, has a Pothole Watch group
that monitors and reports deteriorated neighborhood streets to city
authorities.

Willingness to invest in EOC or developmental activities can also be
undermined by deliberate, conscious efforts not to spend because of the
lack of immediate effects from this effort. This problem is exacerbated by
two factors. First, some EOC investment is relatively unremarkable and
unseen to the public (underground, out-of-sight); and second, effects of
negligence may not be noticeable for many years. The President's 1978
National Urban Policy Report acknowledged the first concern: "Failure to
keep up a city's infrastructure is often a politically less sensitive action than

cuts in the workforce" (U.S. President 1978, 94). A planning commissioner of Allegheny County (Pennsylvania), commenting on deteriorating sanitary sewer lines, said: "Not only is [the sewer problem] a tough problem to get a handle on, . . . but because it is underground and unseen, it doesn't have as much impact as other problems" (*Pittsburgh Post-Gazette*, 18 April 1979). Interviews and conversations with officials indicate that among all mechanisms that hold down total spending, limiting infrastructural outlays usually has the least immediate repercussions: city employees seldom lose jobs, perceived necessary services are not cut back, officials aren't blamed for callousness towards the poor. The effect of limiting infrastructural expenditures is almost imperceptible. Over time, however, it may create problems. The trick is predicting when these problems will occur. Some water lines are over 100 years old and in no need of repair. Others are much newer and in dire need of attention. The gamble taken by city officials is that the effect will be not immediate but long-term.

Then, too, there is the complicating effect of federal requirements. In order to receive federal grants, requirements are often attached to the receipt of aid which increases outlays primarily in general staff areas (McGowan and Stevens 1983). When funds are required to be spent for, say, planning or budgeting activities, total available funds are reduced, and infrastructural or EOC activities are thereby limited. Willingness of city officials to fund EOC activities therefore depends on a complex interaction of factors including social and political pressure, lack of immediate or visible benefits, and federal compliance. All funding decisions require trade-offs among these factors.

One way to examine such trade-offs would be to study the city's decision-making process — an approach we do not use (for a study on infrastructural decision making, see Sanders 1984). Rather, as a way of measuring a city's willingness to invest in its developmental or EOC activities, we separate city expenditures into two categories, EOC (developmental) and SOC (antidevelopmental), and compare longitudinally the relative and absolute emphasis placed on these two categories of activities. This comparison of actual outlays reflects *ex post* internal decisions about the relative priority of EOC and SOC expenditures, as well as implicit trade-offs between the two categories.

Operationalizing EOC/SOC

In this section, we investigate the trade-offs between EOC and SOC expenditures and relate our findings to the theoretical justification for the establishment of these categories. Before we begin, the terms need to be clearly operationalized. We have defined EOC, or developmental activities, as "primarily oriented toward the support of directly productive activities or toward the movement of economic goods" (Hansen 1965, 50). Those activities include roads, bridges, and transportation facilities; water and power; communications facilities; sanitation and sewerage services. SOC encompasses those activities which are primarily social in their orientation or, more generally, it comprises "those services without which [economic] activities cannot function" (Hirschman 1958, 83). Such social activities include health and welfare, fire and police protection, public housing, and education. These categories of expenditures parallel closely the departmental or functional accounts as reported by the Bureau of the Census. Aggregating functional expenditures as EOC or SOC is therefore a fairly straightforward procedure. A city's EOC outlays are operationalized as comprising the following entries in *City Government Finances* (U.S. Department of Commerce): *highways, airports, transit, parking facilities, water transport, sewerage, sanitation, natural resources, water, gas, electricity,* and *urban renewal.* SOC is aggregated according to the following categories: *library, public welfare, hospitals and health, police protection, corrections, protective inspection, fire protection, parks and recreation, housing, financial administration, general control,* and *general public buildings.* These last three entries were not previously cited as examples of SOC because of their managerial characteristics. Paul Peterson (1981) refers to such activities as allocational, a kind of safe, middle ground between developmental and redistributive policies. We include them as SOC activities in the interest of typological consistency, because these activities do not "support directly productive activities" in the same manner as roads and sewers. We do, however, acknowledge the point that good management enhances the efficiency of both EOC and SOC activities. (For a discussion of this issue, see *National Journal* 1983, 820.)

Further, we recognize that some categories might be included as both EOC and SOC. For example, fire and police protection may support directly productive activities, yet we classify them as SOC (following Hansen 1965). Their exclusion from SOC activities would change the results of our analyses only minimally. Thus, we keep them under the SOC rubric. The same can not be said of education. Education is a big-ticket item in cities that have it under their jurisdiction. It dominates the other SOC categories to such an extent that we exclude it, in order to make it possible to focus on variations in the other activities' expenditures.

With these rather tentative operationalizations, we now turn to the data. Census data has provided the categories necessary to compare SOC and EOC outlays. In order to trace the trend of these expenditures over time, we collected data and grouped them according to their purpose (EOC or SOC) for the years 1957 through 1981 or 1982. First, to measure the trade-offs between the two groups of activities, we calculated a ratio of EOC to SOC expenditures for every year of the study period. This ratio indicates the relative emphasis of EOC to SOC activities, or the results of the trade-offs between the two categories. Further, the trend—should a trend be discernible—in the ratio longitudinally indicates the direction the trade-offs may take in the future. In other words, the absolute ratio is not interpreted, but the trend and direction of the ratio is analyzed. Second, we plotted the slopes of the expenditures (SOC and EOC) against time. This is intended as an aid to understanding the trends and trade-offs, by facilitating comparisons between the steepness of the EOC and the SOC slopes. These statistical exercises should indicate the EOC or SOC orientation of city officials. Both of these exercises provide some insight into the history of allocating funds to EOC and SOC activities.

Results of EOC/SOC Trade-offs

As one indicator of the trade-offs between EOC and SOC outlays, we regressed EOC and SOC expenditures on time to compare the slopes or the rates of increase in EOC outlays and SOC outlays over time. The expenditure data were transformed logarithmically, making the relationship with time linear. Table 4.1 presents the logged coefficients for time by both SOC and EOC outlays for each city. The purpose of the table is to understand which group of activities, EOC or SOC, increased faster. For Baltimore and Des Moines, the slopes are almost identical. For the remaining cities, SOC outlays increased at a much faster rate than EOC outlays from 1957 through 1978–79. This observation is especially noticeable for Newark, New Orleans, St. Louis, and Seattle, where the rates of increase for SOC outlays were nearly double those of EOC outlays. Over the study period, then, SOC outlays appear to fare better, relatively speaking, than EOC outlays. The implication is that political pressure, conscious decisions, a greater willingness to increase SOC outlays, federal compliance, and/or immediate visible benefits conspired to increase SOC outlays at faster rates than EOC.

However, in the last few years of the study period the trend begins to reverse. The case-study cities begin to increase EOC expenditures at a faster rate than SOC expenditures. This reversal in trend is clear in the EOC/SOC ratios for each city as presented in figures 4.2 through 4.10. The downward trend apparent for eight of the nine cities (i.e., SOC outlays increasing at a faster rate than EOC outlays), begins to change for Baltimore around 1972, Des Moines in 1972, Hartford in 1978, Newark in 1975, New Orleans in 1975, Pittsburgh in 1977, St. Louis in 1976, and Seattle in 1980. In Dallas, however, the trend has not reversed; SOC has retained about the same proportion of the city's budget. For all U.S. cities, the pattern has been that until 1972, SOC received increasing shares of the budget. This leveled off until 1977. Since then, a dramatic shift has taken place whereby cities, nationwide, have transferred increasingly larger pro-

Table 4.1   Regression coefficients for EOC and SOC by city, 1957–1979.

City		Logged Regression Coefficient (variable year)*
Baltimore	EOC	0.08098
	SOC	0.08418
Dallas	EOC	0.07461
	SOC	0.10909
Des Moines	EOC	0.08291
	SOC	0.08843
Hartford	EOC	0.07801
	SOC	0.09218
Newark	EOC	0.04532
	SOC	0.07156
New Orleans	EOC	0.05474
	SOC	0.09521
Pittsburgh	EOC	0.03675
	SOC	0.05550
St. Louis	EOC	0.03937
	SOC	0.06575
Seattle	EOC	0.05340
	SOC	0.09601

*Statistically significant at the .01 level.

Source: Authors' calculations based on data from the U.S. Department of Commerce, *City Government Finances* (1957–80).

portions of their budgets toward EOC activities (see figure 4.11).

In terms of relative trade-offs between EOC and SOC outlays, these trends imply that after years of favoring SOC, cities began to favor EOC in the mid-1970s. This suggests willingness to invest for developmental purposes at the expense of SOC activities. Several reasons might be offered for this shift in emphasis. First, the riots and discontent of the 1960s forced cities to respond with programs designed to accomplish social purposes. Second, federal programs initially made it easy for cities to develop social programs for the disadvantaged. However, this legacy of federal intervention has unwittingly exacerbated the shift away from SOC activities.

During the 1960s and early 1970s, federal programs and grants-in-aid increased for both SOC and EOC programs. By the late 1970s and early 1980s, federal funding for both SOC and EOC activities decreased. Cities adjusted to SOC cutbacks from Washington by reducing total expenditures for SOC activities, which affected beneficiaries directly, and led to the release of employees who administered those programs. The result, obviously, was that the governmental structures designed to administer the SOC

Figure 4.2   Ratio of EOC to SOC Expenditures for Baltimore.

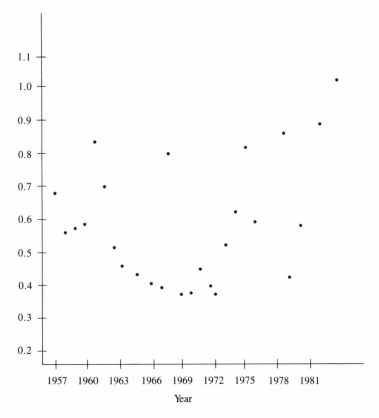

Source: Based on data from the U.S. Department of Commerce, *City Government Finances* (1957–82).

activities were dismantled, and services were reduced or eliminated entirely — with little or no repercussion to cities' budgets. However, infrastructural programs that were aided by the federal government were less likely to shut down completely, even though EOC programs were reduced (e.g., EDA, CDBG, UDAG, EPA). The difference is that even though federal capital programs were reduced, the governmental structures and services could not be curtailed (or at least not as completely as with SOC programs). Because of this, a direct budgetary impact was felt by cities. Cities could not just ignore segments of sewer lines because there were no operating funds available for maintenance activities. Federal funds for infrastructure services can be curtailed, but cities are still required to maintain the capital plant. Federal disengagement thus has a budgetary impact. Continued city funds are required because the physical infrastructure still exists. Of course,

Figure 4.3   Ratio of EOC to SOC Expenditures for Dallas.

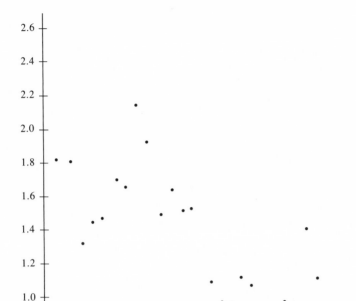

Source: Based on data from the U.S. Department of Commerce, *City Government Finances*
(1957–82).

poverty, hunger, inadequate housing, and other social problems also continue to exist, even when federal funds are gone, but in a budgetary sense,
it is easier to eliminate social programs than to reduce infrastructural
outlays. Federal cutbacks, then, forced cities to decide between caring for
their physical assets and caring for their disadvantaged. It appears that they
chose the former.

A third reason for the funding shift is a profound philosophical shift that
began in the mid-1970s. Most officials whom we interviewed thought that
the time had now come to refocus the city's activities on economic growth
rather than on social programs. The previous emphasis had been on directly
improving social programs, which city officials now see as only palliatives
to social problems. The shift is now toward improving the economic development prospects of the city, which in turn will benefit, or trickle down to,

Figure 4.4   Ratio of EOC to SOC Expenditures for Des Moines.

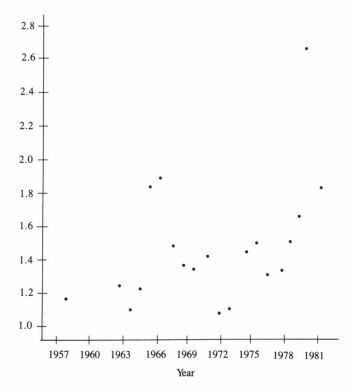

Source: Based on data from the U.S. Department of Commerce, *City Government Finance* (1957–82).

the poor. One sewerage official complained that new industrial development would be virtually impossible to sustain because of lack of capacity in the interceptors. Another official claimed that water and sewer expansion is a prerequisite to any economic growth. Others pointed to the need for better streets to serve business and industry. Most of the city officials concurred that infrastructure and developmental activities have been slighted in the past, and that now that the problem has been recognized, such activities should increase. The data bear this out.

Thus, in most of the case-study cities, emphases have shifted, priorities have reversed, and the trade-offs have been made. Cities are now pursuing a course of action that places higher priority and greater funding levels on EOC categories than in the past.

Figure 4.5   Ratio of EOC to SOC Expenditures for Hartford.

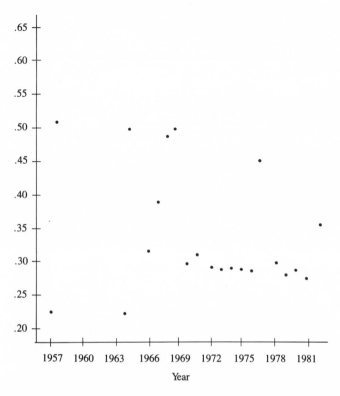

Source: Based on data from the U.S. Department of Commerce, *City Government Finances*
(1957–82).

Refining the Conceptual Framework

Now that we have established the empirical fact that cities have been
more concerned with SOC than EOC activities until relatively recently, we
can address ourselves to the utility of the typology adopted herein. We
propose to challenge the implicit assumption that some municipal activities
are developmental and others antidevelopmental. In reference to our opening passages in the first chapter, which contain the assumption that infrastructure possesses properties that attract industry, is there sufficient empirical evidence to indicate whether the timing of governmental activity (as a
leading or lagging sector) is important in the process of economic growth?
If we assume that governmental activity precedes private investment, is this
timing coincidental to private-investment decisions or are those decisions

Figure 4.6   Ratio of EOC to SOC Expenditures for Newark.

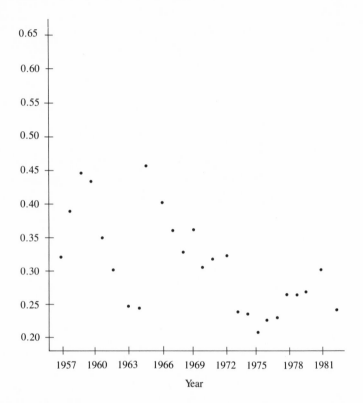

Source: Based on data from the U.S. Department of Commerce, *City Government Finances*
(1957–82).

induced by government actions? Finally, to what extent do public-sector activities make a difference in the development process?

Leading/Lagging Sector Theories   Few scholars have moved beyond assuming that a relationship exists between public and private outlays. Most studies on the interaction between the public and private sectors assume that local economic development was promoted by public programs. Individual case histories or "success stories" (Clark 1981, fn 1) have overshadowed any real analysis of this assumption, which, unfortunately, has contradictory causal applications. If firms locate or expand or if employment or income increases in a certain area after a public program is initiated, the assumption is that the public program caused these outcomes; on the other hand, if firms locate or expand at a site and then public programs are

Figure 4.7   Ratio of EOC to SOC Expenditures for New Orleans.

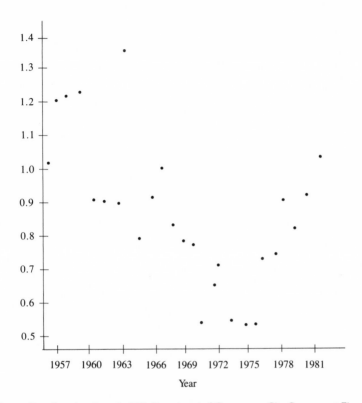

Year

Source: Based on data from the U.S. Department of Commerce, *City Government Finances* (1957–82).

initiated to service the firms, the assumption is that the private sector caused the public sector to respond. Both assumptions, although contradictory, can be espoused by the same individual. And both assumptions have support in the literature.

Take the second one, namely, that public facilities and programs follow private investment or location decisions. It finds considerable support. For example, Judd and Collins argue:

The assumption is that (private) investment leads to increased jobs and an increased tax base. This . . . raises . . . incomes . . . and improves the public services . . . Higher incomes lead to increased spending and consumption . . . Better public services result in public improvements and neighborhood services. . . . Increased spending and consumption creates a favorable business environment which, of course, encourages investment, and on around the cycle again (1979, 182–83).

Figure 4.8   Ratio of EOC to SOC Expenditures for Pittsburgh.

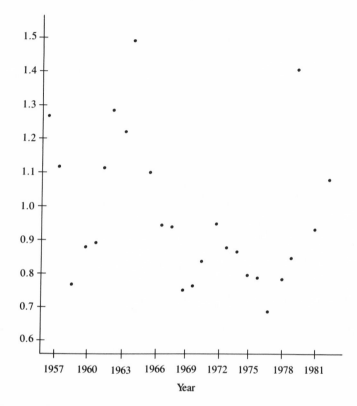

Source: Based on data from the U.S. Department of Commerce, *City Government Finances* (1957–82).

This model suggests that public services follow private investment decisions and income growth (although the authors view it differently—a point we will discuss later). Such a model is even better stated in the industrial location and urban economics literature. Industrial location studies introduce a spatial dimension to economics that has been overlooked in classical economics. Losch recognizes that firms locate in areas where transportation costs are minimized if all other costs are equal. Each firm then produces for a certain market area that is determined by the interaction of the supply of raw materials and the distribution of population. Lampard outlines what he considers to be the three primary costs that act as determinants of industrial location: "(1) input costs—defined as labor, material, fuel, water, taxes, insurance, weather conditions, political milieu, etc.; (2) transport costs—defined as the price of a composite input of services

Figure 4.9   Ratio of EOC to SOC Expenditures for St. Louis.

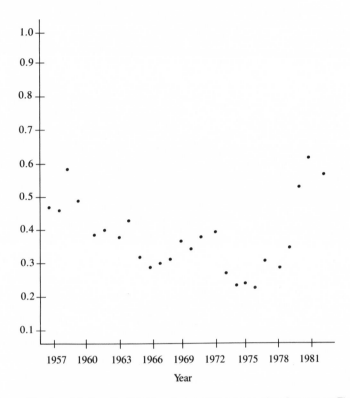

Source: Based on data from the U.S. Department of Commerce, *City Government Finances*
(1957–82).

necessary to move labor, material, equipment and products; (3) economies (and diseconomies) of agglomeration and deglomeration—defined as a set of relatively localized scale economies that may be (a) 'internal' to the firms, (b) 'external' to the industry at a particular location, or (c) 'external' to the locality itself" (Lampard 1968, 89).

The relative weight assigned to each cost varies from industry to industry. Other industrial location studies emphasize different factors. For example, McMillan summarizes the literature of basic factors in location decisions in this manner: "These factors are usually markets; raw materials; service facilities or industries; labor supply and wage levels; electric power and fuel (low cost); transportation facilities; good plant sites; experience of existing industries; tax environment; attitude of local people toward (a) labor unions, (b) company policies, (c) politics; pleasant living conditions; schools and

Figure 4.10   Ratio of EOC to SOC Expenditures for Seattle.

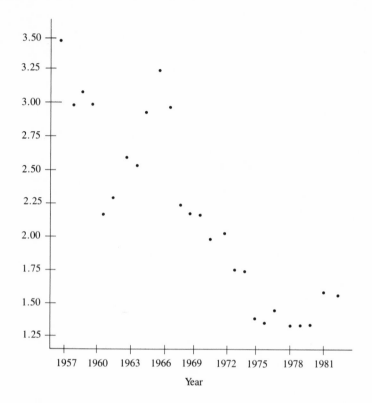

Source: Based on data from the U.S. Department of Commerce, *City Government Finances*
(1957–82).

churches; good housing; moderate climate; recreational facilities; good city
planning and zoning; lower construction costs; cooperation of local citizens;
and adequate water" (1965, 239). Neutze (1967) reduces the list to four
major determinants: natural features, costs of transport and communication,
production technology, and demand patterns. Dean (1972–73) adds that
industrial location studies must differentiate between small firms, which
tend to rely on personal factors and on the owners' "contact space" (i.e.,
knowledge about other areas), and large firms, which tend to rely more on
professional and scientific appraisals.

Fuchs (1962) estimates that between 1929 and 1954 approximately
one-third of the geographical shifts in manufacturing employment could be
attributed to natural-resource endowment and raw-material availability.
Another one-third of the geographical shifts was due to labor costs, and the

Figure 4.11   Ratio of EOC to SOC Expenditures for the United States.

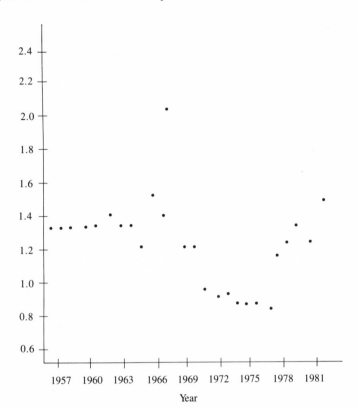

Year

Source: Based on data from the U.S. Department of Commerce, *City Government Finances*
(1957–82).

remaining one-third resulted from a change in demand for products. Chinitz
(1960) argues that the decentralization of industry, or industries' relocation
or birth in areas that have had a low concentration of industry, is a natural
process because transportation costs are minimized when the distribution
of industry corresponds to the distribution of population (1960, 114–128).
In his estimation, the role of agglomeration economies became increasingly less important in the location process as transportation costs became a
smaller proportion of total production costs. Hoover (1948) and others also
emphasize the importance of transportation costs. Isard (1956), Hoover,
and others emphasized industry-specific locational determinants. There is
an infinite array of combinations and permutations of these theoretical
determinants of industrial location, and the results of studies are directly
related to the mix of factors selected by the researcher to be investigated.

In most of the industrial location studies, the provision of government services (save education) is scarcely noted. Researchers speculate that level of taxation may affect the decision to locate because it affects production costs, but usually conclude that its effect is minimal. McMillan (1965) disagrees and tries to demonstrate the saliency of taxes. His study relies on case studies of six firms, all of which decided to locate or expand on the basis of tax rates or other government-controlled variables. His point is interesting, but because he relies on a tiny, nonrandomly selected handful of cases, he has not invalidated the findings of other studies that relegate government-sponsored activities to a low position in the overall location calculus. Wasylenko (1981) reviews the impact of taxes on industrial location and concludes that taxes are inconsequential in interregional location, but may have an intraregional effect. Richardson's excellent and comprehensive review of the urban and regional economic literature (1979) does not even include a discussion of the urban public sector's role in the decision of firms to select one site over another.

Many of these studies run into difficulty in disaggregating government activities from other variables. For example, transportation access includes availability of highways (a government activity), railroads (usually a private concern), and waterways (a function of natural-resource endowment and government and/or private development). Availability of materials usually refers to natural-resource endowments and proximity to same, and exploitation of these resources, usually by private firms or in the case of water by the public sector. The problem, then, is not that the literature fails to recognize the myriad determinants of industrial location, but rather that it cannot disaggregate the impact of public sector activities on industrial location. Older cities' inherited capital stock may indeed be an advantage for attracting economic activity, but it does not follow from the industrial location studies that it is critical. Indeed, labor and land costs, proximity to markets, and transportation costs are more often cited as the major determinants of location than the public capital stock.

The urban economics literature likewise tends to ignore the effects of public capital investment on economic growth and development. Couched generally in marketplace terminology, this body of literature suggests that urban public sectors spend resources that reflect demand for public services (Richardson, 1969). As demand increases, the public sector must respond to it or face the possibility of losing firms and individuals to competing regions, cities, or suburbs. This view is presented most forcefully by Charles Tiebout (1956). He argues that if costs (i.e., taxes) at one location exceed the benefits at that location for any taxpayer, then the taxpayer, which includes firms, will "vote with his feet" by moving to another area that provides a better package of services for an acceptable cost. Cities adjust the composition of their activities because they strive toward some optimum size. For our purposes, Tiebout's hypothesis is inadequate because of the aggregation of the analyses. The package of services that a taxpayer consumes does include the infrastructure along with other publicly provided activities. But this package also includes an amount of education, streets, police and fire protection, judicial activities, and other goods and services. If residents and firms decide to leave the area because of an unacceptable package of services, the extent to which one part of that package, e.g., infrastructure, has influenced that decision is unknown. Therefore, older cities in possession of an inherited capital stock may or may not have any advantage in competing for economic activity.

This is not to suggest that EOC or development policies do not contribute to economic growth and development. However, the ability of EOC to attract industry has not been demonstrated in the industrial location or urban economics literature. The argument of this literature is that firms select sites or decide to expand primarily on the basis of land, labor, and capital costs; transportation; natural-resource endowment; and market areas. Government activities that already exist are not considered. This does not mean that they are inconsequential, but rather that they have not been shown to be determinants of location or expansion.

From this perspective, the public sector's responsibility is to respond or react to investment decisions by private firms. Providing public services (both EOC and SOC) in the expectation that firms will locate or expand is foolhardy unless there is good reason to believe that firms will select that locality based on other determinants of location. On this basis, many declining cities would be well advised not to augment their public expenditures with the expectation that such outlays will lead to private investment decisions. At a conference on the New Jersey Infrastructure Bank, a representative of Jersey City (a city in dire fiscal straits) commented: "We're simply trying to stay afloat. Decisions are made independent of private investment decisions" (Moore and Beer 1984).

This "wait-and-see" approach has certainly not been adopted by at least two other major professions that contribute to the urban economic development debate, namely, developmental economics (Third World or underdeveloped regions) and the planning profession.

Recommendations for public intervention to stimulate economic development span the spectrum from providing few goods and services to building industrial and commercial complexes. Among the developmental economists, Waterston (1966) proposes that the public sector promote or lead economic development primarily by providing social and economic infrastructure. Hirschman (1958, 1967), Myrdal (1957), King and Barkin (1970), and others (inter alia, Friedmann 1966; Mountjoy 1966), agree but recommend that the state be even further involved by engaging in directly productive industrial and agricultural activities. Hirschman's (1958) backward- and forward-linkage industrial development approach requires the public sector to identify sectoral and geographic growth areas and then to produce appropriate goods and services. According to Hirschman, this activity in turn will stimulate private investment and economic development in an orderly manner by inducing investments in one of the linkage industries. Public investments can be thought of as an indication to the private sector of where the government expects economic growth to occur. Thus, government stimulates private investment and economic growth by reducing risks for the private sector.

Urban planners have much the same outlook. Given certain long-term goals, planners identify the optimal mix of resources to attain their goals of rational and orderly development. These plans indicate to the private sector where they might receive aid, where public investment most likely will be made, and thus, where some of their costs and risks might be reduced.

Both developmental economists and planners, then, believe that public-sector strategies and activities promote growth and induce investment. From this perspective, the public sector, by its actions, can lead the private sector in many of its investment decisions. Indeed, most governments accept the premise of their leading role as the underlying rationale for the involvement. Most state and local governments utilize a variety of "Locate Here!" strategies in the hope of attracting private investment. These strategies include low-interest loans, industrial development and revenue bonds, sale/lease-back arrangements, land assemblage, etc. However, as Goodman (1979) notes, the competitive edge provided by these economic development strategies is often reduced or eliminated by neighboring states' provisions of similar incentives. Thus, the assumption that properties of the public sector's programs do induce firms' behavior patterns can result in bidding wars. The most recent evidence is the current battle for the siting of General Motors Saturn plant. The Committee for Economic Development averred that "if the local public sector is unwilling to make a sufficient commitment of money and effort, its community will lose position to those that respond more energetically" (1982, 2). Grants, subsidies, loans and other programs proffered by local governments take on the characteristics of incentives to the private sector in their location or expansion decisions. As Tobin states, "The private sector will not become involved [in the redevelopment process] unless enough guaranteed incentives, and subsidies, are given by the public sector" (1983, 474). According to Judd and Collins, cities are "forced to pursue economic growth" (1979, 183), which seems to suggest that city policies can attract private investment. The public sector, then, is viewed by these scholars as leading private investment decisions.

But even though Tobin appears to believe that public activities lead private investment, he is explicit in identifying the power of public programs to attract private investment as nothing more than an assumption of his model. Clark questions this type of assumption by asserting that "if government spending is going to be decreased anyway, it might be best to cut those programs that attempt to stimulate the private sector. Their benefits are questionable and largely undemonstrated." (1981, 3). And Pagano raises the policy implications:

Should the public sector respond to private sector signals, assuming that the public sector "lags" private sector investment decisions? Or, should the public sector invest at higher levels so that increased supply induces more economic activity to take advantage of the [subsidized] slack, assuming that the public sector "leads" private sector investment? (1982, 132).

These authors do not question that certain public programs are necessary to the process of economic development. However, they point out that the literature has not adequately determined whether public activities labeled "developmental" actually precede or follow private investment.

The crucial importance of the answer to the leading/lagging question should be apparent. If it can be demonstrated empirically that public programs lag private investment, then declines in developmental or EOC outlays should not have a major impact on the development potential of an urban area.

EOC as Stimulative of Economic Development Even if it can be determined that the provision of public programs precedes private investments, that timing does not necessarily mean that the private sector was induced to invest. For example, let's assume that the public sector leads private investment. On the basis of this finding, a growing city should increase its package of EOC activities. However, that action should not be misconstrued as necessarily confirming the theory that it has stimulated private investments. Private investments may have been forthcoming anyway. If so, the timing of public-sector activities coincidentally preceded private investment, but they did not induce the private sector response. Furthermore, although the curtailment or cutback of public investments might retard economic growth by creating "bottlenecks," their provision does not necessarily lead to stimulation (Pagano and Moore 1983).

A variable in the private sector's decision-making processes which has not been well-studied is the influence of public sector developmental activities. Until more is known about the effects of public actions on investment/expansion decisions, assumptions will still be relied on. However, there are some instances where the possibility of a stimulative impact has been enhanced by program requirements. For example, the Urban Development Action Grant (UDAG) program requires a "but for" clause in the agreement before federal funds are released. The but for clause states that without federal UDAG funds, the recipient would not be able to proceed with the project; or "but for" UDAG, the project would not be feasible. Under these circumstances, it seems clear that a public-sector action does stimulate private investment. However, little evidence exists to substantiate that the but for clause has been effective. Webman's study of UDAG calls for more research to determine whether "the UDAG program makes a difference in investors' decisions about where to locate new or expanded enterprises" (1981, 201–2). And few other programs require anything like a but for clause.

Thus, the question is whether public activities actually induce private investment just because they precede private investment temporally. Even a programmatic requirement such as the but for clause still may not induce private investment, although its curtailment may disrupt current economic activity (e.g., bridge closings). Thus, all we can say for certain is that the ability of developmental policies to attract investment has not been established sufficiently to recommend appropriate actions for municipalities.

Making a Difference　Most scholars and public officials assume that public programs do make a difference to private investments. Downtown redevelopment efforts, often instigated by elected officials and funded at least in part from public resources, have made central business districts more attractive to shoppers and shopkeepers alike. UDAGs and more recently CDBGs are credited with leveraging hundreds of millions of private investment dollars. Incentive packages lure firms and businesses. At least, those are some of the conclusions of case studies (Webman 1981; Freiser 1982; Fosler and Berger 1982). From a common-sense perspective, subsidies and other forms of direct and indirect aid ought to be appealing to a prospective firm. From an analytical perspective, it may not suffice. Few success stories have a control group so that the true effects of public programs can be scientifically compared. Newly renovated downtown areas might have become lucrative to private developers if they were to have deteriorated to a point that the cost of renovation and land/building purchases would have been competitive with alternative arrangements. Downtown redevelopment efforts might have been realized (eventually) without the active participation of city governments.

The response by many is "Of course not!" Without downtown redevelopment and convention center construction, consumers would have gone elsewhere, tourists would not have come, businesses would not have invested. We're not so sure. It might be that public involvement has accelerated urban redevelopment, but the important question is whether such redevelopment would have occurred without it. Success stories might have been successes without public intervention. The fact that some activity and employment take place because of these projects does not provide a rationale for authorizing the activity in the first place. The question we pose is not a "was-it-worth-it?" question from a benefit/cost, fiscal impact, or public finance perspective. Instead we ask whether activities of a developmental or EOC nature actually bring about private investment.

New Directions

In light of the questions and assumptions we have raised above, the expenditure data on EOC and SOC activities should be reexamined. Let's assume that public investments do precede private investments. Under such an assumption, shifting city priorities away from developmental or EOC activities as evidenced in the era prior to the mid-1970s (figures 4.1 through 4.10) should be counterproductive to the cities' developmental capacity.

On the other hand, if we assume that public investment is preceded by private investment, then declining public investment would not be viewed as antidevelopmental. Under this assumption, one would argue that cities have not been sufficiently spurred or induced by the private sector to invest, or that cities have had insufficient private investment or pressure to justify public investment. Alternatively, one might argue that pressure was exerted to increase SOC outlays in order to quell riots and social unrest, or, as O'Connor (1973) suggests, for legitimation purposes. The cities in our sample, therefore, reacted rationally to their economic environments by responding to weak or nonexistent signals, and spent less for developmental purposes. Thus, based on this operating assumption, alarm about the deteriorating infrastructure in the U.S. is misplaced. Infrastructure investment (a component of developmental activities) has simply not been perceived as necessary by city officials who are looking for private sector signals. Once those signals appear, investment and repair will be forthcoming.

It certainly seems to be true that the potential infrastructure problem was recognized by city officials much earlier than 1981 with the original publication of *America in Ruins* (Choate and Walter 1981) and other tracts on the decaying infrastructure. Cities had already chosen to increase expenditures for developmental functions by the mid-1970s. Within the context of this study, we cannot be certain whether this renewed interest in developmental activities was based on a reaction to private demands or in anticipation of such demands. However, based on conversations with city officials, we are convinced that they were keenly aware of the trend away from infrastructural activities during the previous fifteen or twenty years; and that this awareness translated into greater relative expenditures for developmental functions in the mid-1970s.

Thus, the mid-1970s signalled the beginning of a fundamental shift in cities' priorities and assumptions about economic growth and development.

Prior to that time, most of the cities in the study favored social or SOC activities. Whether they consciously subscribed to a lagging sector theory of growth, we are not sure. Nor are we sure whether they had been greatly concerned about their developmental role. Indeed, many cities have a parochial, "beggar-thy-neighbor" definition of what constitutes development. They view the attraction of industry or firm as developmental, even if the firm relocates from an adjacent suburb and provides no additional employment to the region. Nevertheless, since the mid-1970s city officials have accepted (at least implicitly) the leading-sector theory; that is, if sufficient public investment and developmental activity are provided, then private investment will soon follow.

We would argue that cities are now proceeding as if they do indeed lead economic growth, a decision that is manifest not only in the recent EOC expenditure gains relative to SOC outlays, but also in pronouncements of public officials. A supervisor of an Iowa County stated it bluntly in an interview: "We're not going to get economic development when you rob the infrastructure of funds. You won't see economic development in Blackhawk County, Iowa if I can't run a sewer line out to the new industrial site." Or, according to the Speaker of the New York State Assembly: "Public spending for roads, bridges, and mass transit may be even more useful than new tax cuts in attracting business to New York State." Other officials tend to agree.

This apparent relative shift toward developmental programs in the past five to ten years at the municipal level has profound implications. Besides the question we raised earlier about whether this shift is warranted from a theoretical perspective, a major question about the role of cities in the intergovernmental system arises. For although cities' behavior may not be affected significantly by the receipt of federal capital grants, cities' total spending certainly is affected by federal participation. If federal programs were designed on the basis of assumptions that are no longer held by local officials nor reflected in their developmental programs, the partners of the intergovernmental system may be working at odds with one another. The result may be deleterious to development of our cities. Indeed, the national urban policies of the Carter and Reagan administrations may have had little if any positive impact on the developmental capabilities of cities—except possibly for the UDAG program, which might be an important exception, but which is also minor, compared to all expenditures on federal developmental activities. The following chapter explores urban policies with an emphasis on the cities' changing priorities and assumptions about urban economic development.

5. National Urban Policies
Exacerbating the Infrastructure Problem

Recognition of the deteriorating quality and consequent low productivity of America's infrastructure comes, unfortunately, at a time when several forces are working against the resolution of the problem. First, fiscal pressure at all levels of government has led to crisis management of the infrastructure. Second, although federal involvement tends not to alter city budgetary behavior, the antimaintenance bias in existing programs has not encouraged cities to meet their repair needs. This negative federal influence is exacerbated because cities have built and must maintain infrastructure systems larger than they would have built without federal subsidies. Third, fiscal pressures have forced local governments to decide between the competing needs of social programs and developmental programs. One encouraging sign for the infrastructure is that there has been a subtle, but consistent, change in the perception of many local officials as to the proper developmental role that cities and urban governments should perform, and a recognition of the economic consequences of poorly upgraded or maintained infrastructure. Cities increasingly have played an active role in pursuing: (a) policies oriented toward providing fiscal escape valves for overburdened tax bases; and (b) policies oriented toward capturing and promoting economic development. Finally, there has been a philosophical shift in the federal government's perception of what its role ought to be in the intergovernmental system. Government, it would seem, can play an active leading-sector role in economic development, and the provision of infrastructure is part of that role. It is somewhat ironic that this apparent new local public awareness comes at a time when the federal government and federal policy are in a period of contraction. Thus, different perceptions of the role of the public sector in economic development lead federal and local governments in different directions.

   This chapter will explore the realignment of federal responsibilities, particularly during the past several years. A principal focus will be on exploring the Carter and Reagan responses to localized developmental needs with regard to infrastructure. In this context, our concern is the degree to which the recent orientation of federal policy has been attuned to the setting of local priorities. We then examine how localities have developed options both for meeting fiscal demands and, more important, for attracting and promoting private economic development. Given the current climate of federal policy, what choices are available to localities in the pursuit of their developmental goals? We review several options for cities on the assumption that if government can play a leading-sector role, then investment in the physical plant, or economic overhead capital (EOC), as we have defined it, makes sense. Finally, we address the question of what an appropriate intergovernmental partnership should be, and argue that the current trend in federalism may be inappropriate. One of the key issues in the bifurcation of federal and local developmental goals is an argument about the merit of public-works investment. Some think that public works are nothing more than "makework activity," the result of "pork barrel politics." In this view, the value of public-works investment is solely the immediate employment consequences. If it is true that government does not lead private investment and economic development, the argument against pork barrel has some merit. However, we will argue that the utility of public capital investment is more than politics as usual, that there is productivity to such investment, that the need for a sound economic base involves such investment, and that the public sector can pursue developmental goals in a planned fashion.

Changes in Federal Grants-in-aid

Total federal aid to states and localities for fiscal year (FY) 1982 amounted to approximately $88 billion, a dramatic decline in absolute terms from the FY 1981 total of almost $95 billion. That decline of more than 7 percent can be represented in several ways. As a proportion of total domestic spending by the federal government, federal grants-in-aid declined to one-sixth, the lowest proportion since 1965. As a proportion of total state and local expenditures, federal grants-in-aid declined to 22 percent, the lowest level in a decade. As a proportion of the gross national product (GNP), federal grants-in-aid fell to less than 3 percent, again the lowest level in a decade (table 5.1).

However, the 1982 declines were not the beginning of a new trend. In fact, since 1978, federal grants have declined in relation to all three measures noted above: in relation to total federal expenditures, in relation to state and local expenditures, and as a proportion of GNP. As one study notes:

During the last half century, the federal government's role in the American intergovernmental system almost continuously expanded, through social programs, fiscal transfers, and mandated standards for state and local performance. This participa-

Table 5.1 Historical trend of federal grant-in-aid outlays
(fiscal years; dollar amounts in millions).

	Total grants-in-aid	Federal grants as a percentage of			
		Budget outlays		State and local ex-penditures[2]	Gross national product
		Total	Domestic[1]		
Five-year intervals:					
1950	$ 2,253	5.3%	8.8%	10.4%	0.9%
1955	3,207	4.7	12.1	10.1	0.8
1960	7,020	7.6	15.9	14.7	1.4
1965	10,904	9.2	16.5	15.3	1.7
1970	24,014	12.3	21.3	19.2	2.3
1975	49,834	15.4	21.5	23.0	3.3
Annually:					
1976	59,093	16.2	21.9	24.2	3.5
1977	68,414	17.1	22.9	25.9	3.7
1978	77,889	17.4	23.1	26.8	3.7
1979	82,858	16.9	22.5	26.3	3.5
1980	91,472	15.9	21.2	26.2	3.6
1981	94,762	14.4	19.5	25.0	3.1
1982	88,194	12.1	16.6	22.1	2.9

1. Excludes outlays for the national defense and international affairs functions.
2. As defined in the national income and product accounts.
Source: U.S. President, Office of Management and Budget 1984, Special Analysis H.

tion peaked in 1978, when federal grants and revenue sharing comprised almost 27 percent of all state and local government expenditures. . . .

Although the federal role continued to expand during the early 1970s, the advent of revenue sharing and block grants set up an undertow that promises to become the dominant current in intergovernmental finance. By the end of the decade, as federal fiscal problems worsened with inflation, federal aid was decreasing (National Research Council 1981, 54–55).

During the Carter administration, and more precipitously during the Reagan administration, the nature of the federal-state-local partnership changed greatly as a consequence of the philosophies and actions of the New Federalism (of the Nixon years), the New Partnership (of the Carter years), and the new, New Federalism of the Reagan years. As the National Research Council study notes: "One of the major objectives of the realignment of responsibility in the federal system is to transfer discretion over how resources are used to those officials who are directly responsible to the

Table 5.2   Composition of grant-in-aid outlays
(fiscal years; dollar amounts in millions).

		Composition of grants-in-aid		
	Total grants-in-aid A	Grants for payments for individuals B	Grants for capital investments[1] C	Other D
Five-year intervals:				
1950	2,253	1,257	484	512
1955	3,207	1,623	820	764
1960	7,020	2,479	3,321	1,220
1965	10,904	3,931	4,985	1,988
1970	24,014	9,023	7,053	7,938
1975	49,834	17,441	10,867	21,526
Annually:				
1976	59,093	21,023	13,475	24,595
1977	68,414	23,860	16,109	28,445
1978	77,889	25,981	18,316	33,592
1979	82,858	28,765	20,043	34,050
1980	91,472	34,174	22,464	34,834
1981	94,762	39,934	22,132	32,696
1982	88,194	40,744	20,480	26,970

political communities in which the expenditures occur" (1981, 61). It is not clear, however, that the politics of devolution has led to appropriate transfers in financial resources, management capabilities, or altered federal requirements. Without such transfers, the developmental capabilities of urban governments may be short-circuited.

Although the decline (in constant-dollar terms) in total federal aid to states and localities has been dramatic over the past five years, federal aid for public capital investments presents a more mixed picture. As we noted in chapter 3, federal grants-in-aid (in current dollars) specifically for capital purposes grew constantly from 1960 through the early 1970s. As George Peterson notes: "Since the mid-1970s, federal capital assistance has been the principal engine of whatever growth (in nominal terms) there has been in state and local capital spending" (1984, 12). Table 5.2 demonstrates the trend throughout the period. Federal capital assistance (column C) grew from $3.3 billion in 1960 to almost $11 billion in 1975, and

are of State & local capital expenditures financed by		
Grants-in-aid E	Own-source revenues F	Column C/A G
8.4%	91.6%	21.5%
8.3	91.7	25.6
23.9	76.1	47.3
24.8	75.2	45.7
24.6	75.4	29.4
25.8	74.2	21.8
31.1	68.9	22.8
41.1	58.9	23.5
41.1	58.9	23.5
40.0	60.0	24.2
39.6	60.4	24.6
39.0	61.0	23.4
37.9	62.1	23.2

cludes a small capital grant that is included as a payment for individuals.
e: U.S. President, Office of Management and Budget 1984, Special Analysis H.

remained a relatively constant share of state and local capital spending at approximately one-fourth of the total. However, it should also be noted that construction grants as a share of total grants to states and localities fell from approximately 47 percent in 1960 to less than 25 percent in the mid-1970s (column G). This changing proportion does not so much reflect a change in commitment to capital assistance, as it does the sheer growth of federal social programs.

From 1976, federal capital assistance marginally increased its share of total grants-in-aid, but total federal grants-in-aid in constant-dollar terms began to decline. These trends in federal capital grants are presented in table 5.3 in current dollars, in constant dollars, and as a percentage of GNP. Again, the meaning of this changing proportion is at first deceptive. At first glance, one might argue that this increasing relative share of federal capital assistance is indicative of renewed commitment to economic development programs. However, we suggest that this really is more indicative of the

Table 5.3 Federal grants for state and local capital investment.

Purpose	1955	1960	1965	1970	1975	1980	1981	1982
	(in billions of current dollars)							
Transportation:								
Highways	0.6	2.9	4.0	4.3	4.6	9.0	8.8	7.7
Urban mass transit and airports	*	0.1	0.1	0.2	1.0	2.6	3.1	2.9
Community and regional development	*	0.1	0.6	1.6	2.5	5.8	5.6	5.2
Natural resources and environment	*	*	0.2	0.4	3.8	4.9	4.5	4.1
All other	0.2	0.1	0.2	0.6	0.5	0.2	0.2	0.3
Total grants for physical capital investment	0.8	3.2	5.1	7.1	12.4	22.5	22.2	20.2
	(in billions of constant 1972 dollars)							
Transportation	1.0	4.6	6.0	5.2	4.0	5.5	5.3	4.6
Community development and housing	0.1	0.2	0.9	1.9	1.8	2.7	2.5	2.2
Natural resources and environment	*	0.1	0.2	0.4	1.7	2.3	2.0	1.8
All other	0.3	0.2	0.2	0.6	0.4	0.1	0.1	0.1
Total	1.4	5.2	7.3	8.1	7.9	10.6	9.8	8.7
	(as a percentage of GNP)							
Transportation	0.16	0.60	0.62	0.47	0.37	0.45	0.41	0.35
Community and regional development	0.01	0.02	0.09	0.17	0.17	0.22	0.19	0.17
Natural resources and environment	0.01	0.02	0.02	0.04	0.15	0.19	0.16	0.13
All other	0.04	0.03	0.02	0.06	0.04	0.01	0.01	0.01
Total	0.22	0.67	0.76	0.73	0.73	0.87	0.77	0.66

Source: U.S. President, Office of Management and Budget 1984, Special Analysis H.

fiscal impacts of an emergent federal philosophy that had begun earlier but found fruition by 1976. It does *not* mark a resurgence of interest in capital programs; it is the beginning of devolution and contraction generally. By 1978, federal capital assistance had peaked at more than 41 percent of all state and local capital spending and has since declined as a share of state and local capital spending (column E of table 5.2). This presents a problem because states and localities had become dependent on the federal government not just in terms of total expenditures, but specifically for the fulfillment of a large portion of their role in capital formation.

Let's review briefly the major observations above: (1) Federal grants for capital spending increased steadily from 1960–1975, but only as a reflection of the general increase in federal aid; as a proportion of federal grants-in-aid, capital grants remained relatively stable during that period; (2) There has been no appreciable change in the amount of constant-dollar capital grants in the post-1975 period; (3) As a share of state and local capital spending, however, federal capital spending has increased, peaking in 1978, and declining since.

The picture grows more gloomy. Since 1978, federal capital spending has declined only slightly as a proportion of state and local capital spending, and between fiscal years 1980 and 1982, the value of federal capital grants has dropped even in nominal terms (U.S. President, Office of Management and Budget 1984, Special Analyses D and H).

The federal government has become the dominant partner in the process of local capital formation in terms of the sheer magnitude of its contribution to capital formation. Yet the role that the federal government has played as a partner in state and local economic development (as measured in terms of grant assistance) has followed a rather unpredictable course. A report by Morgan Guaranty Trust puts it well:

Poor performance of public investment during the past decade also reflects swings in federal grants-in-aid—opening the spigot, turning it off, then opening it again. . . . The resulting yo-yo pattern in federal grants . . . has disrupted capital spending in countless communities (July 1982, 13).

These swings were evident in Nixon's impounding of funds for sewer and highway construction, the growth of GRS after 1973, congressional passage of local public works programs in 1976, and later cutbacks in local public works programs.

One clear example of this schizophrenic approach to federal intervention is the matching portion required by many federal programs. For example, prior to 1965, federal regulation of and investment in state and local water and water pollution control was virtually nonexistent. From 1965 to 1968, the federal match was 33 percent; states and localities were required to raise the additional 67 percent. For local governments this usually meant the issuance of general obligation or revenue tax-exempt bonds. From 1968 to 1972, the federal match was 55 percent, thus lowering substantially the local financial match. However, federally imposed standards were initiated during this period. Because of these standards, even though the local match was lower, total investment needs were larger. The 1972 Federal Water Pollution Control Act Amendments created a 75 percent match, but with the added match came added standards. The total investment needs rose again, leading to long-term financial commitments by states and localities as new bonds were issued to meet new standards on projects and to meet entire new system requirements. And in 1981, the federal government's contribution to water and water-pollution control funding shifted again. In the words of one official in New Jersey's Department of Environmental Protection, "the bucks came to a screeching halt," with the Reagan administration's rescinding of large amounts of funding intended for water-pollution control,[1] the lowering of the federal match (back to 55 percent) for FY 1985 and beyond, and the congressional stipulation that grants be applied only to current population needs.

State governments have responded to this erratic federal behavior equally erratically. As a result, localities have been faced with two unpredictable partners in a three-way relationship. As federal grants increased, state-level grants have often decreased in percentage terms. In New Jersey, for example, state participation in water-pollution control declined from a 25 percent grant match in the late 1960s to 15 percent (through 1976), to an 8 percent loan to localities for the near future. As a result, the local match requirement has shifted from 20 percent to 10 percent to 17 percent to a current 37 percent, with a possible increase to 45 percent in the future. George Peterson reinforces the image of the erratic partnership in a discussion of Local Public Works programs: "The experience with special public works programs has been even more volatile. The obviously temporary nature of these 100 percent federally funded programs caused state and local governments to postpone or cancel their own capital spending in anticipation of the receipt of federal dollars. One study concludes that the net effect of federal public works grants was to depress state and local capital spending and to cause the postponement of as much as $22 billion in capital expenditures . . . , although this estimate seems implausibly high" (1984, 118).

Shifts in the Federal Role

We turn now to an evaluation of recent events with regard to federal participation in local capital financing during the years of the Carter and Reagan administrations. Our purpose in this section is not to provide a comprehensive description and analysis of intergovernmental relations during the period. That analysis is well beyond the scope of this study. Rather, we seek to expand the argument of the previous chapter and ask the question: to what degree has federal policy in recent years reflected what appears to have been a shift in local perceptions of the developmental role of cities?

The 1970s brought a dramatic growth in the amount of federal financing of state and local capital expenditures. In addition, a number of important shifts occurred in the programmatic and functional purposes of federal capital grants. Until the 1970s, the major federal capital programs financed the federal highway system. As a result of expansion in the Federal-Aid Urban Systems (FAUS) program and the Interstate Highway System, cities benefited both directly and indirectly. Of course, the impact on cities in terms of other effects—such as facilitating bypass of urban areas, allowing for suburban manufacturing and transport facilities, or making possible central city flight—was not always positive. During the 1970s, several programmatic shifts occurred. First, new purposes for federal capital grants were identified, particularly in the areas of wastewater treatment and aid for public-transit systems. Second, in some programs (highways, bridge systems) there was a shift of some funding from new construction to repair and rehabilitation.[2] In a broader sense, there was a philosophical shift in the perception of the role of the federal government in capital financing. This shift was most clearly manifest in an increased discretionary role for states and localities in the use of federal funds, and in the increased targeting of federal aid to cities with fiscal constraints or large needy populations.

Carter and the Federal/Local Partnership On 27 March 1978, President Carter offered Congress and the nation his "proposals for a comprehensive national urban policy." Six months later, the Department of Housing and Urban Development issued the first *National Urban Policy Report* (U.S. President 1978).[3] This document, together with several previous monographs prepared by the President's Urban and Regional Policy Group, provides a clear indication of what still is probably the most comprehensive statement of national urban policy in the United States to date.[4]

Essentially, four principal emphases emerge from these documents, and most particularly from the *Report*. These four emphases can be identified in the nine discrete "Urban Policy Objectives" in the *Report*. (1) Three of these objectives—improving local management capacity, encouraging state participation in assisting urban areas, and stimulating local investment —are directed toward restructuring of the decision-making process of and participation in urban policy formation (i.e., the acclaimed New Partnership). (2) Three objectives—providing employment opportunities, access, and social services for the urban disadvantaged—focus on targeting programs for the urban poor. (3) One objective—improving the physical and cultural environment—extends the quality-of-life emphasis of recent years. (4) The final two objectives—fiscal relief for distressed cities, and incentives for urban private investment—respond to issues of urban economic development and fiscal strain.

In many ways, the Carter urban program continued the gradual disengagement of the federal government from urban problems that had begun under the Nixon administration. Nixon's New Federalism was replaced by Carter's New Partnership, but the perception of an altered public role for the federal government continued. Perhaps the principal manifestation of this subtle shift in the perception of how best to resolve America's urban needs came in the form of several new programs of the 1970s, continued or begun under Carter, including General Revenue Sharing (GRS), the Community Development Block Grant (CDBG) program, Urban Mass Transit Administration (UMTA) grants, and the Urban Development Action Grant (UDAG) program, as means by which federal assistance to localities would be managed. But, as Bahl has noted, "federal policy toward the state and local government sector during the decade was ambiguous, often contradictory, and generally ill-conceived" (1981, 8). We would argue that Bahl's statement particularly applies to those portions of these and other programs that focus on the financing of state and local infrastructure and economic development. Several principal elements of these programs are worth highlighting.

In the adoption of the UDAG program in 1977, and in modifications to the CDBG program, one sees a noticeable attempt by the federal government to provide economic stimulus to localities. In the case of the UDAG program, the intent was to stimulate employment and increase tax revenues in distressed areas principally through the stimulation of private investment and privatized economic activity (Webman 1981). Clarke and Rich note that the UDAG program contains an "explicit statement that the public sector cannot and should not attempt urban economic development and revitalization without significant private sector involvement" (1982, 4). Similarly, the CDBG program suggests a shift in the federal/local partnership, particularly in the 1977 amendments to the Housing and Community Development Act. Michael Reagan and John Sanzone note that, with regard to the targeting component of the 1977 amendments: "The tightening of the formula for improving the targeting of CDBG funds and HUD's more assertive role are counter-balances made necessary by a critical flaw in the philosophy of the New Federalism: the assumption that decentralization will lead to the achievement of national goals without strong federal supervision" (1981, 144). We would go one step farther. The altered federal role in supervision suggests a change in the willingness of the federal government to involve itself in local activities.

The 1977 amendments to the CDBG program introduce greater flexibility for private-sector involvement, and have the effect of "reducing the burden of performance monitoring on the part of the federal government and shifting the burden to the recipient jurisdictions" (Reagan and Sanzone 1981, 146). This shift is not only a statement of "hands off" with regard to local discretion; it hints at a broader hands off with regard to local economic development generally. The hint becomes a formal shout in the report from the President's Commission for a National Agenda for the Eighties, which, in a concluding section entitled "Redefining the Federal Role in Urban Policy," states in bold print: "The federal government can best assure the well-being of the nation's people and the vitality of communities in which they live by striving to create and maintain a vibrant national economy characterized by an attractive investment climate that is conducive to high rates of economic productivity and growth and defined by low rates of inflation, unemployment, and dependency" (1980, 101). Thus, the emphasis on local economic development becomes, at best, a corollary to national economic development. And the report goes further, again in bold print for emphasis: "Federal urban policy efforts should not necessarily be used to discourage the deconcentration and dispersal of industry and households from central urban locations" (1980, 104). The federal policy has not only lost an urban/local focus; it clearly suggests no need to pursue local/urban development at all! And finally: "A people-to-jobs strategy should be crafted with priority over, but in concert with, the jobs-to-people strategy that serves as a major theme in current federal urban policy" (1980, 106). Here we see the full extent of the new federal/local partnership. Issues of targeting, job creation, and economic stimulus increasingly are phrased in terms of non-federal involvement.

The subtle shift in the ideology of federal/local relations in the Carter years is also reflected in the general objectives of federal programs. In 1977, the administration introduced three economic stimulus grant programs to reduce unemployment and promote economic recovery: (1) from 1977 to 1980 the federal government expended $600 million, $3.1 billion, $1.7 billion and $0.4 billion in local public works (LPW); (2) in the same years, $2.3 billion, $4.8 billion, $3.3 billion, and $1.8 billion were expended in temporary employment assistance (CETA); (3) in 1977, $1.7 billion were expended on antirecessionary fiscal assistance (ARFA), and in 1978, $1.3 billion. Although the economic recovery or stimulus package of these years was an obvious boon to state and local governments, pumping as much as $9.2 billion to state and local governments in 1978, the programs had another clear objective. As Reischauer notes: "Not only did the federal government assist state and local governments in performing nonfederal functions, but it also used these governments as contractors to fulfill federal objectives such as stabilizing the economy" (1981, 22–23).

Finally, the shift in federal perception is evident in the Carter years in the continuation of the GRS program, which from 1972 to 1980 provided states and localities with more than $6 billion per year. The spread effects of these general purpose grants implies a shift in the allocation of responsibility for decision making not only for economic development, but more generally. The GRS allocation forces local governments to assume greater responsibility for decisions with regard to social programs. Ironically, the use of both GRS and CDBG funds by local governments in recent years suggest their increasing awareness of the need to promote economic development locally: larger and larger shares of both programs have been reported to have been used for infrastructural purposes (Reagan and Sanzone 1981; Nathan, Adams, and Associates 1977). Thus, although the federal government increasingly has abrogated its responsibility for promoting local economic development, local governments have increased their responsibility in recent years. Not only does the debate focus on what the public role is, but also on who should perform it. Again, the President's Commission is instructive: "The federal role in urban policy should allow for the sorting out of roles and responsibilities among levels of government and between the public and private sectors" (1980, 108).

Reagan and the Abrogation of Federal Responsibility If the hint of this abrogation can be seen in Carter's policies, a clear statement of abrogation is explicit in Reagan's policies. The recent changes in the role of the federal government in state and local capital financing augur poorly for the present and future, particularly for fiscally stressed cities. The shifts that have occurred can be seen generally in two ways: (1) reductions of federal aid to states and localities suggest an objective of limiting the federal role to financing only those capital facilities with truly national impact, while encouraging states and localities to finance the rest; (2) federal actions in fiscal policy have limited the capacity of local governments to finance capital investments. We explore each of these shifts briefly.

Impacts of Changes in Capital Grants. Total federal grants-in-aid to states and localities declined by $6.6 billion between FY 1981 and FY 1982, the first year of the Reagan administration. Although reductions in grants for capital purposes were not as large as originally proposed, the significance of cuts are being and will be felt in many ways. In a study of reductions in domestic federal spending, Ellwood (1982) notes that there are major differences between Congressional Budget Office (CBO) current policy baseline estimates for unchanged federal policies and actual 1982 budget authority. In those grant programs that affect capital expenditures, Ellwood's findings can be summarized as follows: (1) Increases in budget authority from CBO baseline estimates occurred in only two areas of relevance: federal aid to highways increased by 5 percent to $8.3 billion; wastewater treatment grants increased by 50 percent to $2.4 billion.[5] (2) Declines in budget authority occurred in all other capital grant programs: highway safety grants for operating and capital purposes declined by 137 percent, possible only because of rescissions in prior-year contract authority and dramatic declines in current-year authority; CDBG grants for operating and capital purposes declined by 13 percent; EDA grants declined by 66 percent; UMTA grants were cut 31 percent; UDAG budget authority was cut by 34 percent; and housing assistance grants for capital and operating purposes were cut by 43 percent.

These various cuts had impacts both for state and local governments

(Nathan, Doolittle and Associates 1983, 55–56). From the perspective of state governments the principal impacts were not profound. These were: a decrease in CDBG funding with, however, an increase in the small-city portion and cuts for larger jurisdictions; an increase in highway funds with a significant increase to follow because of the five cent per gallon increase in the federal gasoline tax; relatively large cuts in energy conservation, land and water conservation (small programs), and in EDA grants, although in the last case the impacts will not be felt immediately. Although changes in federal grants did not have immediate profound effects on state governments, as Nathan, Doolittle, and Associates note, "despite the relative stability of funding of federal capital grants compared to operating and entitlement grants, changes (or even the prospects of change) in these programs were very important at the state level in 1982. There was considerable apprehension that future cuts in capital grants to states would occur as the Reagan administration continued its efforts to reduce the federal deficit" (1983, 56).

The impacts of changes in budget authority for federal capital grant programs were more profound for cities. It is true that for smaller jurisdictions, where dependence on federal grants generally is less significant (Nathan, Doolittle, and Associates 1983, 152), changes in capital programs were not severely felt. CDBG funding was even increased, although the increase may be completely offset by the potential impact of large cuts in EDA funding. For larger jurisdictions, however, the 1982 cuts had more negative consequences. First, uncertainty based on initial Reagan attempts to cut more deeply into these programs, public perceptions of the scale of the cuts, delays in appropriations, city fears of possible rescissions during the year, and the perennial uncertainty surrounding discretionary grants that vary annually made cities reluctant to commit new resources (Nathan, Doolittle, and Associates 1983, 112). In the wastewater treatment program, reductions in budget authority occurred, late appropriations in state review of projects led to uncertainty among localities, and there was a reduction in the federal match (for 1984). For UMTA programs, 1982 budget authority was reduced drastically (31 percent, although the subsequent raising of the gasoline tax aided in capital improvements in 1983 or 1984).

However, the most significant impacts for larger jurisdictions came in the form of cuts in both UDAG and EDA grants, and a reduction in the entitlement portion of the CDBG program, which provides funds for larger jurisdictions. In each of these programs, federal funds to promote local economic development were cut, at a time when localities were seeking to expand their developmental activities. In response to these cuts, the search for creative alternatives to achieve local economic development and to finance capital improvements has been increasingly seen.

Fiscal Policy and Local Capital Formation. The impact of the philosophical shift in the Reagan administration is not only felt specifically in federal grants policy, but also more generally in domestic fiscal and monetary policy. President Reagan has consistently insisted on the need for stimulation of investment in the private sector. Much has been written about the Reagan administration's emphasis on supply-side economics through programs aimed at rapid depreciation allowances, liberalized investment tax credits, enterprise zones, reduced federal intervention, and so on. Supply-side economics, in a broad sense, refers to an approach to economic growth that emphasizes capital investment, technical knowledge, and entrepreneurial activity. In addition to the qualitative dimension of unleashing entrepreneurial spirit and behavior, the key to the Reagan administration's approach is investment in both human and capital resources: more efficient equipment and a more skilled labor pool will raise the marginal productivity of labor and lead to higher levels of economic growth. This perspective, together with fiscal conservatism, comprise the fundamental building blocks of President Reagan's long-term economic recovery program.

The debate over whether the supply-side perspective has been operationalized properly centers on how best to encourage investment, unfetter capitalism, and encourage risk takers. Much of the programmatic content of Reagan's domestic fiscal policy brings into question whether Washington's principal public partners—state and especially local governments—will be able to assume the role being thrust upon them by the federal government under the guise of the new New Federalism. It is also questionable whether they will be able to perform their role in the capital formation process. Much of the administration's devolution of power and effort to stimulate private investment is based on the assumption that local governments will take on the burden of stimulating local private capital formation. Because the supply-side incentives package of the Reagan administration focuses little attention directly on public capital infrastructural needs, local governments are faced with the growing problems of postponed additions, repairs, and replacements to existing public capital stock. Thus, faced with cutbacks in federal aid generally, specific cuts in capital grants-in-aid, and an increasing blurring of federal urban policy goals as part of national economic recovery, localities find themselves in the fearful position of "going it alone." Furthermore, many aspects of the Reagan administration's economic recovery proposals have affected local financing negatively due to their impact on debt financing, tax base reductions, and greater financial costs to borrowers who are forced to compete to attract private investors.

Traditionally, borrowing in the tax-exempt market has provided the major source of both state and local financing of capital outlays. The municipal bond market has grown in size and complexity in recent decades, especially in the 1970s. In terms of the size of the market, the growth of long-term debt outstanding for states and localities has grown from $70.8 billion in 1960 to $361.3 billion in 1981 (Board of Governors, Federal Reserve 1982). In the last several years, an increasingly complex tax-exempt market has been created, and radical changes have occurred. The consequence has been an increase in revenue-raising difficulties for states and localities, because of the rapid rise of interest rates, increased competition for investors in the tax-exempt market, the rise of nonmarket altrnatives for potential and traditional investors, and the increased risk associated with a number of borrower issues (e.g., the downgrading of bond ratings).[6] In particular, actions taken at the federal level in a sluggish economy compounded access and finance problems for states and localities through early 1982. An examination of these changes by Petersen and Hough points to these added difficulties: "These difficulties arose in large part from simultaneous changes in the federal tax code, reductions in the federal budget, and the impact of recession on revenues. To these changes, which reduced investor demand for tax exempts while making access to that market even more important, must be added the pressures brought by restrictive monetary policy and a continuing growth in private-purpose tax-exempt borrowing. The latter swelled the supply of the tax-exempt securities in the midst of weak demand for such securities" (1983, 13–14).

Another component of the tax-exempt market is the change in the composition of investors. Historically, the participation of household investors has declined precipitously (from 43.5 percent of total holdings of state and local securities in 1960 to 26.8 percent in 1981), while commercial banks and property and casualty insurance companies have increased their share of the market (from 36.4 percent in 1960 to 65.9 percent in 1981); see table 5.4. However, demand for tax-exempt bonds by the institutional investors "evaporated after 1979 due to poor profitability and the availability of competing tax shelters" (Petersen and Hough 1983, 15). In 1981, households accounted for more than 50 percent of new purchases; in 1982 (through the third quarter), the household sector continued to absorb more than half of new issuances (Board of Governors, Federal Reserve 1982).

This shift, which began in 1979, has accelerated since the implementation of several policies of the 1980s. The clearest examples of policy changes from 1981 were the creation of new individual investment opportunities through the establishment of All-Saver certificates, and the broadened scope of Individual Retirement Accounts (IRAS), at a time when households had become the principal lenders in terms of new purchases in the traditional tax-exempt market. These new alternatives with equal (or better) yields and similar maturities have competed directly for investor dollars.

Furthermore, the creation of special bonds and other tax-exempt borrowing devices, has "jammed" the bond market. Although Congress passed

Table 5.4   Holders of state and local securities by major investment group (billions).

Year	House-holds	Com-mercial Banks	Non–Life Insurance	Corporate Business	State and Local Gov-ernments	Other	Total
1981	$96.8 (26.8%)	$155.1 (42.9%)	$83.0 (23.0%)		$26.4 (7.3%)		$361.3 (100%)
1980	74.2 (22.1)	149.2 (44.4)	81.1 (24.1)	$3.5 (1.0)	$6.5 (1.9)	$21.6 (6.4)	336.1 (100)
1979	71.5 (23.1)	135.6 (43.8)	72.8 (23.5)	3.7 (1.2)	6.2 (2.0)	19.5 (6.3)	309.3 (100)
1978	68.9 (24.0)	126.2 (43.9)	62.9 (21.9)	3.7 (1.3)	7.3 (2.5)	18.5 (6.4)	287.5 (100)
1977	68.6 (26.2)	115.2 (44.1)	49.4 (18.9)	3.5 (1.3)	7.9 (3.0)	16.8 (6.4)	261.4 (100)
1976	70.1 (29.3)	106.0 (44.3)	38.7 (16.2)	3.4 (1.4)	7.3 (3.0)	14.0 (5.8)	239.5 (100)
1975	68.1 (30.4)	102.9 (46.0)	33.3 (14.9)	4.5 (2.0)	5.0 (2.2)	10.0 (4.5)	223.8 (100)
1970	46.0 (31.9)	70.2 (48.6)	17.0 (11.8)	2.2 (1.5)	2.4 (1.7)	6.6 (4.6)	144.4 (100)
1965	36.4 (36.3)	38.8 (38.7)	11.3 (11.3)	4.6 (4.6)	2.2 (2.2)	7.0 (7.0)	100.3 (100)
1960	30.8 (43.5)	17.7 (25.0)	8.1 (11.4)	2.4 (3.4)	2.7 (3.8)	9.1 (12.9)	70.8 (100)

Source: Board of Governors, Federal Reserve System, *Flow of Funds Account,* December 1982.

legislation as early as 1969 to restrict and refine the issuance of Industrial Revenue Bonds (IRBs), state-authorized development agencies now exist in forty-eight of the fifty states. One estimate suggests that new IRB issuances have risen from $1.0 billion in 1975 to $10 billion in 1981 (Vaughan 1984, 190), and may represent as much as 25–50 percent of new long-term financing. Offered at rates below taxable bonds, and earning tax-free income, these bonds again compete directly with local-issued general obligation bonds.

Coupled with changes in the bond market have been changes in the tax code (as the result of both the Economic Recovery Tax Act of 1981 and the 1982 Tax Equity and Fiscal Responsibility Act). For individual taxpayers these actions have reduced marginal tax rates on personal income, reduced the capital gains rate, and offered income shelters (IRAs, All-Saver Certificates, etc.), all of which mean that former tax-exempt municipal bond investors may seek higher-yield taxables (Moore and Pagano 1983).

Table 5.5   Levels and ratios of interest rates, 1978–1982.

Year/Quarter	Bond Buyer 20 Bond Index (Tax-Exempt)	Moody's All Industry Corporate Bonds (Taxable)	Ratio of Tax-Exempt To Taxable (%)
1978 (yr.)	6.07%	9.07%	66.0%
1979 (yr.)	6.53	10.12	64.5
1980/I	8.56	12.80	66.9
1980/II	7.86	12.32	63.8
1980/III	8.79	12.30	71.5
1980/IV	9.61	13.67	70.3
1981/I	9.97	14.09	70.8
1981/II	10.68	14.89	71.7
1981/III	12.03	15.65	76.9
1981/IV	12.59	15.64	80.5
1982/I	12.96	15.95	81.3
1982/II	12.19	15.55	78.4
1982/III	11.06	15.03	73.6
1982/IV	10.14	13.49	75.2

Source: *Resources in Review,* Government Finance Research Center, Municipal Finance Officers Association, as cited in Petersen and Hough (1983, 14).

Similarly, corporate taxpayers may take advantage of rapid depreciation allowances, capital gains allowances, and various leasing tax shelter options rather than seek tax shelters through the tax-exempt market where returns are lower.

The result has been that local borrowers must also raise yields: municipalities in recent years have paid as much as 85 percent of what the Treasury pays for long-term money (up from 70 percent in 1980); interest rates were up to 13 percent as recently as the first quarter of 1982 (as compared to half that rate in 1979); and municipalities now pay 75–80 percent of the costs of comparable taxable corporate bonds (see table 5.5). The fourth quarter of 1982 showed strong recovery of both the long-term and short-term markets. However, because of (1) the dominance of individual investors, (2) the concern over the quality of debt, (3) the presence of so many nonmunicipal alternatives in the long-term market, and (4) the continuing impact of federal policies, it is not clear that the problems of state and local borrowers have truly been ameliorated.

As a result of all these factors, prospects for locally funded public capital investment seem dismal. Localities faced with fiscal problems use their scarce debt capabilities for purposes that may be considered less than ideal public investments (e.g., a movement away from traditional infrastructure purposes). They find themselves less able to compete effectively in a growing tax-exempt market; forced to raise interest yields (and therefore raise future debt service burdens) to compete with taxable corporate bonds; forced to provide tax benefits (in the form of packaged tax reductions or private-oriented subsidies) that further limit current receipts; and/or bound by legal limitations that on the one hand may prevent raising tax rates or total debt, and on the other may tie their own borrowing or taxing capabilities to the federal government—all of this, at a time when federal commitment to capital infrastructure clearly is waning.

City Responses to Declining Federal Commitment

Since the federal government's commitment to assisting cities has waxed and waned during the past several years, city officials must decide whether to maintain service levels or allow them to decline. To the extent that officials choose to reduce the impact of federal cutbacks, they must find new revenue sources to replace federal dollars. Cities proceed in many cases in a "quick-fix" fashion: find untapped revenue sources, experiment with new and unused financing techniques, or raise existing taxes. However, the quick-fix response is gradually giving way to a much broader guaged, development-oriented approach. First, we describe traditional tried-and-true methods of raising revenues. Then, we address the new, emerging issues in municipal capital financing as they relate to economic development.

Fiscal Strategies The tax and expenditure limitation movements as embodied in Proposition 13 (California), Proposition 2 1/2 (Massachusetts), and other legal actions, have coincided with the decline in federal commitments to cities (Matz 1981). Finance officers have been sent scurrying to find every conceivable course of action that might replace lost revenues. Some cities have taxed what was previously untaxed and/or raised the tax rates on already taxed activities. Others have captured some of the urban flight or exurban growth through consolidation and annexation (Fleishman 1977). Others have employed new and innovative methods to reduce fiscal pressure by experimenting with creative financing techniques (Petersen and Hough 1983). In essence, all of these approaches are intended to relieve the fiscal strain felt by cities so that they can maintain their infrastructure investment programs and service delivery systems.

Since Proposition 13, cities have become wary of raising taxes in general, and property taxes specifically. An Advisory Commission on Intergovernmental Relations (ACIR) and Municipal Finance Officers Association (MFOA) study reported that between 1957 and 1977 property taxes fell steadily from 57.1 percent to 42.7 percent of total municipal funding, and that in the four-year period between 1977 and 1980 they fell sharply from 42.7 percent to 35.3 percent (Cline and Shannon 1982, 23). The decline in the relative contribution of property taxes (along with declines in federal and state aid) between 1977 and 1980 was answered in part by modest increases in nonproperty taxes (e.g., income taxes) and other miscellaneous revenues (e.g., interest earnings). By far the sharpest increase was registered in the growth of importance in user charges, which by 1980 accounted for 20.7 percent of total municipal revenues. The ACIR/MFOA survey of 438 cities reported that almost three-quarters of those cities raised the rates on user charges in 1980–81 (Cline and Shannon 1982). Indeed, since Proposition 13, the revenue-raising device most resorted to, and the one that has caused the least protest by taxpayers and city officials, is the user charge.

It should be noted that user charges, which should reflect full-cost pricing of a delivered good or service, need not automatically respond to changes in cost. Several city officials explained to us that the reason for inadequate maintenance of facilities supported by user-charges (e.g., water systems) was the political inability to raise user-charge fees to appropriate levels. In response to this problem, an Urban Institute report recommended that Baltimore establish a sewer and water authority that would be insulated from the political control of city council or other partisan bodies (Humphrey, et al. 1980). This was also the rationale for Boston's creation of an autonomous sewer and water authority. To the extent that a user charge is perceived as a relatively painless revenue-raising device that charges consumers only for what they consume—thereby making it appear fair or equitable, it will continue to enjoy a favored status in city finance offices. However, should it one day be viewed by more city officials as regressive (i.e., by excluding the poor through their inability to pay), its popularity as a revenue-raising device for increasing numbers of activities (e.g., parks) may wane. Currently, as the ACIR/MFOA survey indicates, the perception of user charges as a regressive revenue-gathering method is held by a minority of municipalities (approximately 15 percent of the respondents). For the immediate future, at least, user charges appear to be a mechanism to generate adequate revenues for a variety of activities. This is particularly important because of the constriction of other traditional revenue-raising devices. Given the current popularity of tax and expenditure limitations, property taxes (as well as other forms of taxes) can not be viewed as reliable revenue sources. Furthermore, political feasibility is not the only consideration. Many have argued that increasing taxes drives out middle-income residents, which has a negative impact on the city's fiscal picture.

Annexation retains and expands the tax base by resolving both the problem of middle-income residents voting with their feet and the need for an expanded tax base. Cities that have pursued vigorous annexation policies have been aided, in the short run, on several fronts. Federal capital grant programs aimed at new construction are ideally suited for this growth-oriented strategem. In addition, in some areas land developers in unincorporated sectors construct the infrastructure and pass on these costs to the homeowner. This is particularly true in Texas, where the granting of extra-territorial jurisdiction (ETJ) powers has allowed cities to control contiguous unincorporated areas (Fleischman 1977). Thus, through traditional forms of annexation as well as variants such as Texas' ETJ or the metropolitanization of services, the city gains a larger revenue base and keeps new capital construction costs to a minimum and tax rates low.

Ironically, the use of annexation as a fiscal tool is limited to a rather exclusive club of primarily fiscally solvent cities, most notably to the South and Southwest. Key examples would include most large Texas cities, San Diego, Phoenix, and Oklahoma City (Harrigan 1980, 2). This is not an option readily available to older, fiscally stressed cities that find themselves boxed in by the historical development of autonomous suburban jurisdictions.

However, the annexation strategy so actively pursued by a number of Sunbelt cities is already showing signs of wear. Although obvious short-run advantages have resulted, the longer-run fiscal implications are not as healthy. Massive fringe infrastructural development (as has occurred in Dallas) implies tremendous increases in maintenance costs for the future. Unless there are dramatic changes in the nature of federal grant programs, these costs will have to be absorbed locally and will lead to increasing reluctance to encourage new capital construction. Furthermore, although the strategy has been useful in keeping taxes low, public services have been spread very thin in many locales that have used the annexation option liberally.

The anticipation of these future difficulties has caused some alarm in communities that have annexed great parcels of territory. The mayor of Houston, James McConn, had barely been inaugurated in January of 1980 when he served notice that Houston's favorite device for maintaining its strong tax base—annexation and the expansion of the ETJ—would not flourish under his administration. Similar notice was served by his successor, Kathy Whitmire, who ran for office on a platform of efficiency, austerity, and limited growth.

The argument for metropolitanization of services rests on the logic of increased jurisdictional size to achieve economies of scale and to mitigate the perceived negative effects of the balkanization of jurisdictions. Metropolitanization has been acclaimed due to the need for areawide coordination of service delivery systems, the need for equalizing geographical distribution of burden to consumers, and the need for central-city relief (see, inter alia, Haar et al. 1972; Helfand 1976).

Although touted as an efficient governmental device that will likely reduce fiscal pressures, the likelihood that metropolitanization strategies will be adopted is low. Political pressure and perceived disadvantages of merging with a central city (especially older, fiscally stressed cities) on the part of non-central city residents (whose electoral support is necessary before services can be metropolitanized) augur poorly for the success of the strategy.

Increasingly, cities have turned to private takeover of public facilities and to innovations and gimmickry. These innovations, or creative financing techniques, are defined by Petersen and Hough as "those that differ from the traditional means of raising capital through the sale of standard debt instruments in the tax-exempt security market" (1983, 2). These new relationships are manifest in one of the following ways: (1) shifting the interest-rate risk from investor to borrower; (2) enhancing the creditworthiness of borrowers by shifting credit-related risk to third partners; (3) increasing the type of returns available to investors beyond those available from the regular receipt of interest income payments; and (4) designing instruments so that they appeal to the specialized needs and requirements of certain investor groups (Petersen and Hough 1983, 2). From the city's perspective, these financing techniques reduce costs, thereby alleviating a revenue-generating constraint. This allows public facilities to be maintained at historical levels, even though cities have less money to work with.

It is certainly true that if service levels are not to be reduced as a result of cutbacks in federal programs, a smaller tax base, or other factors contributing to fiscal pressure, then new means of raising revenue need to be found and implemented. Creative financing as well as user charges and consolidation/annexation strategies address cities' fiscal dilemmas first and foremost. They do little to promote economic development, except to the extent that a fiscally sound city may be more conducive to business location and expansion decisions than a city in fiscal chaos. Recently, however, cities have begun to shift their fiscal emphasis from generating revenue to stimulating economic development. Cities that view their role as leading and enticing growth think that the stimulation of development may conduce benefits in terms of greater employment opportunities, more investment, and ultimately increased city revenues.

Economic Development Strategies   The buzzword around the nation today is "rebuilding America, a call for development." Public programs, it is said, should be oriented toward providing a healthy and vibrant economy. Cities should pursue capital investment strategies as part of an overall capital formation process. Some cities attempt to reduce the private costs of doing business at a particular location. Others form a partnership with the private sector. Each of these strategies attempts primarily to improve the economic development prospects of the city, and only secondarily (at best) to address social needs. As one mayor in a precipitously declining city told us, he didn't see that he had the luxury of worrying about the poor in the city. Without economic development, nobody would benefit. His immediate and specific concern is with economic development; his hope is that fiscal and social problems will be ameliorated if the economic health of the city is improved first.

The role of the public sector in the capital-formation process was discussed earlier. Cities are beginning to understand that provision and adequate maintenance of the infrastructure are part and parcel of that capital formation process. This realization represents only a subtle shift in programmatic activities, but a major philosophical shift. To the extent that cities have responded to crumbling infrastructure in the past, it has often been in a manner that suggests that anything in disrepair needs to be repaired. This approach tends to ignore a possibly more important question: does the performance of the capital facility impede or facilitate local development prospects? In other words, can some facilities be allowed to deteriorate with little impact on the developmental capabilities of the city or are they vital to the city's development potential? This *triage* approach to decision making, although not articulated as such by public officials, may in fact be pursued as a result of the heightened awareness of the importance of infrastructure. For if a deteriorating facility demonstrates no potential, why should one expect it to be repaired?

In this vein, the concept of *financing options* takes on a different meaning. Tax and user-charge increases—to the extent that they help improve the performance of infrastructure in its capital-formation role —might be viewed as developmental strategies. If cities view their capital formation responsibilities as vital to augmenting their economic bases and, more important, as leading private-sector investment, then infrastructural projects should be financed to spur economic development, even though the fiscal benefits of such actions may not be forthcoming immediately.

Reducing the costs of doing business might also be a developmental strategy that cities should consider. The employment and income-generating effects of subsidies, loans, tax abatements, and other programs that reduce business costs—that is, publicly provided developmental programs, will eventually benefit the fiscal position of the city, but only because they stimulate development. As one finance officer told us, the property tax abatement offered to a major employer would stimulate economic development in his city and eventually generate additional property tax revenues. The emphasis is on the temporal ordering of the program: first, stimulate economic development, then reap the fiscal harvest. That order is the opposite to that pursued by fiscal officers who look for fiscal release valves first, then worry about what impact those actions might have on migration and economic development. Although we argued earlier that the strategy of subsidizing firms has become so widespread that it is almost impossible to keep a competitive edge, such a strategy certainly is developmentally, rather than fiscally, oriented.

An explicit concern of local governments has been what is currently referred to as the public/private partnership or as joint programs designed to stimulate economic development. Public/private partnership can be viewed as an extension of the public-sector-as-provider-of-subsidies strategy, except that it implies a much more active role for the public sector. Loans and subsidies are only inducements. Public/private partnership requires the public sector to behave as an active partner through joint ventures aimed at developing the city. For example, joint ventures, such as those offered under UDAG, require public and private commitments to each other and to the development project in question. Although UDAG is federally financed, many projects require local governments to improve, upgrade, or construct capital facilities (e.g., parking lots, pedestrian access, public lighting) in order for the UDAG project to proceed. The express purpose of UDAGs is to promote economic development for the long-run economic stability of the locality which will benefit the city's tax capacity.

Inherent in any strategy designed to augment the economic development capacity of cities is the possiblity that outlays for economic development may not reap the anticipated benefits. In other words, there are risks associated with city investments in economic development programs. If industries are attracted or expand, if economic development results, if the public programs lead to private-sector activity, then the risk was worthwhile, and the debts accrued to pay for the public program will be addressed favorably. That form of risk is quite different from the risk associated with fiscal strategies. The risk of assuming fiscal strategies is that people and firms will be driven out by increasing the tax burden, that insufficient revenues will be generated even by creative financing, and that the tax base expansion associated with consolidation/annexation strategies will be inadequate.

The qualitative difference between these two forms of risk should not be understated. They reflect different orientations to the resolution of urban problems that have resulted in part from the tax expenditure and limitation movement, stagnant economic conditions, and a major pruning of the federal government's role in local capital formation. As cities respond to those conditions on the assumption that they lead private investment and urban economic development, they most likely will continue the trend towards prioritizing programs that they perceive as stimulative of economic development first and fiscal health second.

Although there is no doubt that either strategy forces cities to be risk prone, assuming risk is by no means an attractive option. Due to uncertain probability that the selected strategy will produce desired results, cities would prefer not to be forced into selecting a risky course of action. Unfortunately, a safe course of action is not readily identifiable. As a result of federal disengagement and threats to retreat even more in the future, cities must make decisions, and those decisions are inherently risky. The federal cutbacks and resultant local strategies are primarily a result of what we consider to be a bifurcation in the perception of the appropriate role of the federal government by the federal and local public sectors.

A Bifurcation of Roles in Federal/Local Relations

We are presented in the final analysis with incongruities in perception among the various levels of government as to what the infrastructure problem is, how severe it is, and, most important, whose responsibility it is to take action on it. The new New Federalism posits a distinct role for the federal government today, one that addresses itself to the big questions of unemployment, productivity, levels of domestic private investment, etc. From this perspective, federal action should emphasize national solutions for national problems. It is argued that the externalities and spillovers of nationally directed federal programs will ease local problems of development. We have no argument with these perceptions of the big question. However, this raises the question of whether the increasing disengagement of the federal government from state and local problems in the guise of restructuring and reallocating intergovernmental responsibilities is simply a statement that the federal government has no localized role. More worrisome still is the question whether the emphasis on the privatization of development activity is designed to supplant the federal public sector's role in development altogether.

Local governments, confronted with financial constraints and the competing needs for economic development and social welfare, may be unable to assume their increased responsibilities for decision making if such responsibilities are not accompanied by commensurate increases in fiscal resources. As Vaughan notes: "But that decentralization [decision making] must be accompanied by the delegation of necessary powers and the commensurate fiscal resources. For example, the federal government may delegate to states increased responsibility for major transportation programs. But that transfer may be accompanied by other policies to reduce the cost of bond financing and with the delegation of much broader powers" (Vaughan 1983, 174).

In the new intergovernmental relationship, different levels of government, like ships passing in the night, seek different and often contradictory goals. Michael Reagan and John Sanzone, in their classic critique of Nixon's New Federalism, declared that the vision was "simply romantic rhetoric, a facade behind which the national government is to abrogate its domestic role, to reduce its presence to that of an onlooker" (Reagan and Sanzone 1981, 175). The new ships of state (state and local governments) have found themselves foundering in an empty sea. Those who would survive have sought the open sea of the private sector, hanging on to the new (privatized) lifeboats from on high.

It would seem that the intergovernmental system is on the verge of coming full course over the past thirty years, yet with an ironic twist. The major categorical grants of the 1950s and 1960s were initiated as attempts to address: inequalities among jurisdictions in fiscal capacity; different responses of jurisdictions to the needs of the citizenry, particularly the poor; limited administrative capacity of jurisdictions to pursue national policy objectives; spillovers or externality effects that cut across jurisdictional lines (Congressional Budget Office 1983). Through 1960 the bulk of federal grant money was dedicated to two kinds of programs: income securities and transportation. During the 1960s there was a massive increase in federal involvement, in part because cities (and states) were perceived as unwilling to take actions to address "universal problems," i.e., national policy objectives (see table 5.6). The federal perception that urban problems could have spillover effects elicited the federal response. Solutions, particularly for social problems, required direct federal intervention. The federal public sector was seen as a lagging-sector participant in social welfare and economic growth; it picked up the pieces that had resulted from privatized inequality by providing soc, and picked up the infrastructural costs of private economic choices by providing EOC.

Local jurisdictions, either unable or unwilling to play an important role in these activities, were in many ways passive recipients of much of the new money and programs. However, the radical changes in the grant system in the 1970s stemmed in part from an increasing administrative capacity of subnational jurisdictions to deal with some problems, an increasing awareness on the part of subnational jurisdictions that local problems required local solutions, and an increasing awareness at the federal level that national policy required local responses. In many ways, the Urban Growth and New Community Development Act of 1970 was a mandate and a legitimization of these realizations. The emphasis on the need for a comprehensive national urban policy was "a response to two decades of criticism from academic and governmental circles that federal policies had a tremendous aggregate impact on metropolitan areas" (Stowe 1980, 146).

More than a decade has passed since the mandate of the 1970 act. The third *National Urban Policy Report* (U.S. President 1982) culminates in many ways the efforts to undo a national urban policy as well as the gradual but perceptible shift not only in the federal perception of the proper structure of the intergovernmental system, but also in the federal perception of what the infrastructure/urban/development problem is. The current vision explains the federal role in providing local infrastructural needs as "assisting state and local governments to develop more cost effective capital investment strategies. This goal will be accomplished, in part, through gathering

Table 5.6   Growth in Federal outlays for grants,
by function (in billions of current dollars).

Program Areas
Infrastructure and Development
Energy
National Resources and Environment
Transportation
Community and Regional Development
Education, Training, and Social Services
Income Security and Health
Income Security
Health
General Purpose Fiscal Assistance
Other[1]
Total Outlays for Grants

information about innovative, state-of-the-art practices and disseminating the results to State and local government officials." The limited thrust of the federal role comes clear in the continuation of the above statement: "Other aspects of federal aid remain to be determined" (U.S. President 1982). This is a far cry from envisioning the public sector as leading economic development. Furthermore, the 1982 *Report* focuses the entire responsibility for infrastructure development squarely on the backs of states, localities, and the private sector. The discussion in the *Report* expands on such themes as: state and local roles; local infrastructure preservation; independent authorities; state bond guarantees; private-sector initiatives; special assessment districts; and state maintenance and rehabilitation incentives (U.S. President 1982, 34–37).

Roy Bahl, in testimony prepared for the Joint Economic Committee Hearings on the *National Urban Policy Report* points to this weakness in the administration approach: "While much ado is made about public-private cooperation, elimination of cumbersome regulations, and better financial and capital facility planning, it seems pretty clear that the Reagan proposals will further reduce the amount spent by state and local governments on capital investment and maintenance. . . . The President's state-

Outlays			Percentage Growth in Real Terms 1960–1980	1982 Outlays	Percentage Change in Real Terms 1980–1982[1]
1960	1970	1980			
$ 6	$ 25	$ 499	2,420	$ 509	−7
108	429	5,362	1,404	4,871	−17
2,999	4,538	13,087	32	12,171	−15
109	1,780	6,486	1,703	5,379	−24
526	6,390	21,862	1,101	16,589	−36
2,635	5,819	18,495	186	21,930	+2
214	3,850	15,758	1,819	18,839	−3
159	430	8,478	1,441	6,347	−37
264	753	1,445	58	1,559	−9
7,020	24,014	91,472	334	88,194	−17

1. Includes grants for national defense, agriculture, commerce, veterans' programs, administration of justice, and general government.
Source: Congressional Budget Office (1983, viii).

ments, while arguing that public infrastructure investment is important for the country, is silent on how to increase the rate of such investment" (1982, 84).

Ironically, all of this restructuring (read: dismantling) of the federal role comes at a time when cities increasingly recognize and wish to respond to economic developmental needs. The consequences of this bifurcation of local and national perspectives on the need for public-sector leading activity in the area of economic development may be severe. Such consequences may include the following: (1) Bottlenecks in the capital-formation process are likely to occur that can be overcome only by a strong public-sector commitment. (2) To the extent that infrastructure is part of the capital-formation process, those cities unable to finance infrastructure for themselves will fall further behind. "In effect, declining areas will be left to their own devices, with less federal aid and more servicing responsibilities" (Bahl 1982, 85). (3) Awaiting the much-touted long-term benefits of economic recovery and its local spillovers, cities may opt to postpone capital and maintenance expenditures, leading to still further deterioration of these facilities. (4) Alternatively, taxes, fees, and other revenue-generating mechanisms will rise, which, in the short run at least, may drive up business costs and drive out marginal businesses and taxpayers. (5) Conflict and competition over the distribution of scarce resources to finance SOC and/or EOC, now decided upon and expended at the local level, may be heightened, and may even lead to the potential for conflict in the streets.

Throughout, we have argued that recent trends, particularly those encouraged by the current administration, move the federal government in a direction away from what we feel is appropriate for the needs of economic development and the nation's infrastructure. In a broader sense, the Reagan urban policy is not an urban policy at all, "but rather bespeak[s] a more general commitment to a program of economic recovery and revitalization. Thus, stability and predictability in our monetary policy, easing of the burden of federal mandates on localities and regulations on business, a disciplined budget through spending cuts as a precursor to a balanced budget, and tax cuts for businesses and individuals are believed to provide the more potent remedy for all matters of urban distress" (Hicks 1982, 57).

Behind this statement is a belief that any impact on cities is an externality, a by-product of market decisions between consumers and producers. To the degree that externalities generate positive results for cities, all the better. However, if externalities do not prove beneficial, the consequences shall ultimately be borne locally. The federal philosophy never acknowledges what many localities are now eager to suggest: that the separation of local economic development (and as an extension, localized impacts of infrastructural development) from a national recovery package puts the cart before the horse. The consequences of such a reversal may be felt at all levels for a long time to come.

We conclude, then, where we began. There is a need for a recognition, even within the framework of the new New Federalism, that the federal, state, and local governments all have responsibilities for infrastructural development. Instead of simple disengagement (especially at the federal level), we offer below some tentative guidelines for reshaping the intergovernmental dimensions of a public sector committed to leading the economic development process.

Capturing a New Intergovernmental Dynamism

Throughout this volume, we have attempted to weave together several separate but interlocking threads. First, we have attempted to present the infrastructure crisis in a broad theoretical context. We have argued that before this nation can resolve what is to be done about the infrastructure problem, we need to understand the role that infrastructure plays in the economic development process. The economic development function played by public capital investments has to be examined more carefully than it has been in the past.

Second, we have argued that although fiscal constraints are real at the local level, city and other government officials do make, and have made, choices among competing needs. Our attempts to model these choices in the capital budgeting process suggest a need to focus on decisions about competing social and developmental programs, particularly in the context of the intergovernmental system. Finally, we have turned to a historical examination of the degree to which the shifting perception of proper intergovernmental relationships has affected assistance to cities in providing infrastructure, and whether the policies precipitated by this perception have been appropriate.

Disengagement of the federal government will not provide a cure for the nation's infrastructure needs. However, regardless of the role the federal government eventually assumes, action to rebuild America's infrastructure does imply new and expanded roles for states and localities.

Reagan and Sanzone argue for a new era of federalism that shares in part the dominant philosophical image of our times. They recommend a sharing of power and authority between national and state governments, "but that the states' share rests upon the permission and permissiveness of the national government" (1981, 175). We believe that this vision of a new intergovernmental relationship is an appropriate framework for thinking about the infrastructure question. We would add to their framework by suggesting that this permissive relationship rests ultimately on the fact that the federal government cannot abrogate either its financial or its leadership role.

A good rule of thumb for discerning what that federal role should be is offered by Pat Choate and Susan Walter (1981): the level of government mandating a requirement must be prepared to pay for it, and functions in the national interest should not be imposed on inappropriate levels of jurisdiction. "To the extent that state and local jurisdictions are used as vessels of administrative convenience to meet a national need, the federal government must finance the cost from national tax revenues" (1982, 82). Similarly, to the extent that infrastructure serves only a state or local purpose, the same rule would apply: the costs of a facility should be borne by those receiving the benefits. But there is a distributional caveat here. Those costs should be tempered by ability to pay; that is, fiscal capacity must be considered.

This statement suggests a need for expansion of state responsibilities in terms of increased financial management capabilities and programming, and increased commitment of revenues for state and local infrastructural financing. Vaughan (1984) cites one study by the National Conference of State Legislatures that provides a set of possible actions that states might take, ranging from simple technical assistance to the creation of state debt guarantees and infrastructure banks. We include these scenarios in table

Table 5.7   Possible actions for state governments.

Action	Suitable States	Benefits	Drawbacks
Improve technical assistance programs.	All	Facilitate bond issuance and encourage responsible debt management.	Local governments may fear state intrusion.
Create a loan program for water & sewer construction.	All	Stimulate investment in water and sewer facilities and supplement federal wastewater program. Provide loans at favorable rates, particularly for distressed communities and small or infrequent issuers.	Increase state general obligation debt and thereby lower state credit rating.
Create a municipal bond bank.	Rural states with many small issuers	Reduce borrowing costs for small or infrequent issuers.	Local banks, bond counselors, and underwriters may suffer a loss in business.
Earmark state aid for debt service.	States with fiscally distressed communities	Improve rating of bond issues (reduce interest rate) for large, fiscally distressed communities.	Requires a large, permanent state aid program and some state supervision.
Assist local governments with creative financing (through technical assistance programs and enabling legislation.	All	Increase local flexibility. Facilitate use of beneficial techniques, and discourage improper use.	Many techniques are untested. May result in excessive short-term debt, or high interest rates in future.
Create loan programs for energy impact assistance.	Energy-rich states	Finances rapid capital construction in energy boom towns. Supplement to grant programs.	Local governments prefer grants or sharing of severance revenues.
Increase state supervision of local debt management.	States with cities having poor credit ratings or histories of poor financial management.	Encourage responsible debt management, and improve credit ratings.	Increased administrative costs for local governments, possible restriction on local actions.

Table 5.7 (continued)

Action	Suitable States	Benefits	Drawbacks
Guarantee local debt.	Most states	Improve rating on local bonds.	May seriously weaken state credit rating.

Note: The most effective measures are listed first.
Source: National Conference of State Legislatures, Watson, 1982, as cited in Vaughan (1984, 284–85).

5.7. This expanded state role, however, merits monitoring at the federal level. It is conceivable that states will be unresponsive to the economic development and infrastructure problems of local, particularly city, jurisdictions. It is important to remember that part of the reason for the growth of the federal/city partnership in the first place was due to the unresponsiveness of states, particularly in an era of increasing suburban dominance in state governments.

The assertion that "those who benefit, pay" also implies the appropriateness of user fees. First, user fees allow for the incorporation of full-cost pricing, which includes both capital and maintenance costs. Second, user fees are a valid mechanism for incorporating efficiency into the use of a public good. However, our caveat applies. Where user fees deny access of entry to the use of goods or services, as for lower-income populations, provisions should be incorporated to assure access. This could be in the form of direct subsidies, tax abatements, etc.

At the same time, public-sector subsidies of private economic development should be applied with great caution. Most of the costs of infrastructural development, where the benefitter is the private developer, should be borne by those who benefit. This is consistent with our earlier position.

Finally, although we would argue that the dependence of state and local governments on federal aid must be lessened, we nevertheless maintain that the federal government can bear part of the burden, and can certainly coordinate its activities to complement the creative role of states and localities. At the very least, we argue for a more active participation of the federal government in the decentralization of financial and administrative decision making concerning the infrastructure. Discretionary block grants for capital financing, for example, ought to be continued and expanded. However, these discretionary grants must allow states and localities to finance both the maintenance of public works already in place as well as new construction and rehabilitation.

The federal government can also facilitate state and local financing choices by enhancing their capacity to enter the debt market. This can be accomplished in a number of ways: simple subsidies for state and local borrowing; lowering the costs of borrowing in the tax-exempt market; or, as some have suggested, direct interest subsidies to lower the costs of taxable bonds issued by states and localities.

Each of these suggestions indicates the need for the federal government to increase its planning and management capabilities in the financing of public works, and again there are a number of institutional settings within which this could be accomplished. Some have argued for an annual capital budgeting process where Congress would be provided the opportunity to look beyond the immediate horizons of pork-barrel politics to a coordinated national commitment. Others have suggested an expanded institutional role and power for the Economic Development Administration (EDA), which could coordinate these activities. Still others have suggested a new institutional setting: a National Infrastructure Development Bank—perhaps modeled on the Reconstruction Finance Corporation (RFC), or a revolving-loan National Infrastructure Fund to bolster the financial viability and coordination of state and local infrastructure development (National Infrastructure Advisory Committee 1984).

Each of these institutional roles for the federal government has merit, but the real point is that given the need for a renewed commitment to providing infrastructure, the public sector at all levels must pursue economic development in a coordinated fashion and must adopt policies that are creative and proactive rather than merely reactive.

Appendix
Methodology

If infrastructural activities are inefficient, inadequate, or inappropriate, then the infrastructure does not perform as expected. Citizen complaints about potholes or bridge closings would indicate that the infrastructure is performing inadequately. Under such circumstances, maintenance practices are questioned and public-works capital programs are scrutinized. However, our knowledge about appropriate levels of maintenance expenditures is inadequate to make universally applicable recommendations. So many variables affect the performance of infrastructure that general rules and guidelines do not exist (CONSAD 1980).

George Peterson (1976) puts the question of infrastructure performance in the context of the condition of the infrastructure. He develops five indicators of condition that, when taken together, provide some insight into the question of performance. These include (1) direct observation; (2) maintenance and replacement cycles; (3) capital investment needed to improve capital stock to adequate standards; (4) monetary losses due to public-stock condition; (5) data on annual capital and maintenance expenditures.

Because we attempted to collect similar kinds of data at each site, the major problem was collecting cross-city, comparable expenditure and revenue data. Because most cities do not employ standard accounting and recording practices, the task was by no means easy. The Municipal Finance Officers Association (MFOA) has called upon cities to begin standardizing accounting procedures, but at the time of this study, few of the case study cities had. In fact, MFOA standards would not have made our data collection much easier, because MFOA guidelines do not prescribe separating data for maintenance outlays from total operating outlays, or revenue-source data for capital outlays. Because of the differences in reporting standards, it would be useful to highlight some of the main data "cleansing" activities.

Maintenance Expenditures

Most of the cities or special districts responsible for sewer and water systems kept excellent records of maintenance expenditures. Maintenance departments were often clearly delineated in the city's annual financial reports or other internal documents, so actual maintenance expenditures did not have to be reconstructed. These cities also defined *maintenance* in virtually identical terms as encompassing workers, equipment, and labor, and not administrative or clerical salaries or large capital outlays. However, several problems did occur.

First, in three of the cities (Newark, Pittsburgh, Seattle) the special district was responsible for sewage-treatment facilities and main inter- ceptors, and the city was responsible for collector system. In Newark, maintenance expenditure data were readily available; combining both sets of data, then, made Newark's sewer-system maintenance outlays compara- ble to the other cities. Pittsburgh was much the same, except that after 1973, collector-system maintenance was not separable from street and bridge maintenance. The amount of maintenance expenditures lost due to this problem represents probably no more than 5 percent of combined treatment and collection maintenance for the fifteen years prior to 1973. However, we were unable to separate maintenance outlays on Seattle's treatment system from operating expenses. Only maintenance on the collec- tor system is comparable to other cities. One last problem was that, like Seattle, maintenance expenditures were not comparable for St. Louis's sewer system because they too were inseparable from total operating outlays. As for maintenance expenditures on the water system, only in Newark, a city with three independent sources of water supply, and in Baltimore after 1965, were data not able to be disaggregated in a manner comparable with other cities.

A second problem was that maintenance expenditures for Pittsburgh's water system had to be reconstructed due to both an accounting change in 1971 and to the fact that no maintenance line-item existed. Estimates were made by a top-ranking water department official, based on the appropriate contribution of each division to maintenance of the water system.

Other than those specific problems, one general caveat should be issued. Since the implementation of the Public Service Employment (PSE) pro- grams in 1974, the entanglement of federal and local funds for specific activities has accelerated to a point where intensive studies on just the effects of PSE—an effort well beyond the scope of our project—would be required. Even though studies have been undertaken to estimate the impact of PSE on city finances, the maintenance impact has been ignored and very little consensus emerges over the actual effects on city budgets. Although the Nathan et al. (1981) and National Research Council (1980) reports indicated that PSE funds were not substituting for locally generated funds significantly (20–40 percent), in one of our case-study cities, 50 of the 240 positions in one department were CETA employees. Prior to CETA, over 300 positions were fully locally funded. The extent to which that substitutive activity took place in other cities has not been consistently evaluated. However, data collected for wages and salaries that contributed to the maintenance of a particular facility were, to the best of our knowledge, non-CETA funded.

Because maintenance expenditures on water and sewer systems probably do not include CETA funds, the collected data are indicative of the city's or special district's willingness and fiscal capacity to spend for maintenance activities. Further, it should be noted that except in those cities where water and/or sewer systems were city responsibilities, no federal funds could be used for operating or maintenance purposes. They were all to be self-financing principally through user charges and, in a few cases, property taxes. In fact, even city-owned water and sewer systems relied primarily on user charges. Only city sewage-collector systems, when combined organizationally with other public works programs, may receive direct federal funds for maintenance purposes (e.g., via General Revenue Sharing) that were not identified and removed from the data base.

Street and bridge maintenance outlays for the nine case-study cities required little adjustment to make them comparable. Dallas changed its accounting system in 1975, which added some pension and equipment rental costs to maintenance outlays. Thus, maintenance expenditures were estimated between 1975 and 1977 based on the difference between these new entries' estimated costs and total outlays. Des Moines added salaries for administrative and clerical work to total maintenance outlays for the 1957–1962 period. Because that addition was so minor, according to officials, it was not removed from the data base.

Capital Expenditures

Because much of the maintenance expenditure data for most of the cities were in ready-to-use form, the process of collecting these data was fairly straightforward—but rather tedious. Such was not the case for capital outlays. Numerous problems arose here. First, we decided not to collect the data according to the day when a project was initiated or completed, but rather according to when actual expenditures were made—much like the Bureau of the Census. For multiple-year projects, this meant outlays for one project would appear over the entire length of the project, except when no work was performed. Second, because we also wanted to collect revenue-source data for each project (which is the reason for not consulting U.S. Department of Commerce, *City Government Finance*), the usually accessible and reliable capital-projects list or other city records on capital outlays often proved to be useless. Even end-of-year accounting statements did not help, because in many cases federal revenues were projected but not yet received. For example, if a project is to be partially (or fully) funded by a federal grant, the federal agency often pays for the project after its completion or after a phase of the project is completed. In the interim, the contractors require payment for work rendered. Cities often cover this deficit with short-term anticipation notes, usually revenue anticipation notes (RANs). The researcher had to be quite careful not to double count (i.e., add bond funds from the RANs to federal funds). In most cases this problem required the researchers to collect data from a capital-projects list, capital officers' worksheets, contract awards files, and sometimes from annual financial reports, and then to assign actual outlays to the month and year in which expenses actually were incurred. Obviously we attempted to collect data on all projects, but given the incredibly large number of projects, chances are good that we overlooked some projects. If so, it was completely unintentional and hopefully randomly distributed.

Another data-collection problem resulted from the fact that we aggregated annual capital outlays by individual project in most cases. We needed to denote what projects were street and bridge projects and which not, or which were sewer and water projects and which not. Where possible, when projects were not combined, capital outlays for sidewalks, street lighting, or other activities that would not be tied directly to the function of infrastructure (i.e., a foundation for economic activity) were purposefully excluded.

Because of these restrictions on the data-collection process, several data-reconstruction problems should be explained. First, due to the time-consuming nature of this process, capital expenditure data were not always collected for the specified time period, 1957–1977. The data collection began with the most recent year and worked back toward 1957. When it was apparent that the data were too difficult to obtain and reconstruct in the time allocated for data collection, we collected at least ten years worth of data, 1967–1977. That single fact explains most of the differences in the length of time-series data collected among the cities. A second problem obtains because of the combination of revenues under one fund. For example, federal funds to Dallas's water utilities, which includes both the sewer and water system, were combined in a Water Utility Fund account with other fees and charges and intergovernmental revenue. This fund is used for both water and sewer capital projects. The amount of federal funds for only the water system or for only the sewer system was, therefore, not determinable. Furthermore, state and federal aid were combined in the Seattle water department's capital account as well as in the New Orleans sewerage and water department capital account, and elsewhere. Where it was feasible, estimates of the contribution of federal funds were made, e.g., New Orleans; where it was not feasible, it was noted, e.g., Seattle.

Finally, a note on what we decided when the beginning/ending dates of fiscal years were changed. Instead of allocating outlays to a different fiscal year in order to maintain continuity, we accepted the fiscal year changes with no attempt to adjust data. Therefore, Des Moines has an eighteen-month fiscal year (FY 1974), but no FY 1975; Hartford has a transitional three-month fiscal year called FY 1975; Baltimore's FY 1966 is six months. Except for these few fiscal-year changes, annual expenditure entries are truly annual according to the city's fiscal year. Some may be January 1 to December 31 annual outlays, others July 1 to June 30, and so on.

Summary

In sum, five major problems had to be recognized and addressed in cleansing capital investment and maintenance expenditure data: (1) problems of noncomparable functional activities or categories, e.g., some cities' street departments included sewage-collection systems; (2) problems of inseparability of revenue sources, e.g., some funds included revenues from both state and federal sources; (3) accounting changes during the period under study requiring acknowledgment of noncomparable time-series data or reconstruction of the data base; (4) requirements to collect actual expenditures and not intended (budgeted) expenditures; and (5) problems of the fiscal years changing during the period under study.

Finally, we need to mention one additional feature of this study. The nine selected cities were selected because they represented many characteristics of other American cities. Their selection, however, was not scientific or random. They were selected because they shared common problems with many other cities. Our results, therefore, are not generalizable in a statistical sense. Nevertheless, we suggest that because of the diversity of characteristics among the case-study cities (i.e., size of city, city manager/strong mayor form of government, degree of fiscal stress), the results of this effort may be applicable to other cities with similar characteristics.

Notes

Chapter 1

1   There are a few studies that attempt to focus on city-level infrastructural issues, but they tend to be case studies from which broad generalization is very difficult. See for example the series of case studies conducted by the Urban Institute under the direction of George Peterson (1982). See also the work conducted by CONSAD (1980). In each of these endeavors only a selection of city activities and facilities were examined.

2   At the time of the initial field research both authors were employed by CONSAD Research Corporation. However, neither CONSAD nor the U.S. Department of Commerce, for whom the initial study was done, are responsible for conclusions reached in this study. The nine cities were Baltimore, Dallas, Des Moines, Hartford, New Orleans, Newark, Pittsburgh, St. Louis, and Seattle. The cities were selected to reflect some variance of conditions that would seem to affect fiscal capacity and the maintenance and investment conditions of infrastructure. See the appendix to this volume, CONSAD (1980), and Pagano (1980) for more details.

3   There is an interesting parallel to the argument made here within the neo-Marxist literature on fiscal crisis. See for example the early and well-developed argument of O'Connor (1973).

4   A number of technical studies on performance criteria do exist and have been used. For example, for street and bridge performance standards, the Federal Highway Administration publishes an inventory and manual (U.S. Department of Transportation 1975). Similarly, the Environmental Protection Agency is required to provide a biennial "needs survey" in compliance with the Federal Water Pollution Control Act (U.S. Environmental Protection Agency 1982). For an excellent review see CONSAD (1980, vol. IV, app. B), and Dames and Moore (1978).

5   This data collection was conducted while both authors were employed by CONSAD Research Corporation. A more detailed description of the selection process, which included a preliminary telephone survey of twenty-seven cities, is provided in CONSAD (1980). That report also provides detailed descriptive case-study reports on the nine cities. See also the appendix to this volume for further description of the data collection.

Chapter 2

1 Among the exceptions are work done by George Peterson (1976, 1978, 1981, 1980–82, 1984) of the Urban Institute, John Petersen of the Municipal Finance Research Division of the Municipal Finance Officers Association (1976), and Terry Nichols Clark and associates (Clark and Ferguson 1983) at the University of Chicago. Of course, crisis cities such as New York City or Cleveland have been examined. But, this has occurred precisely because these cities are perceived as unique.

2 We use the term tax burden throughout this section, but a more appropriate term might be "municipal public sectors' cost burden per capita," because (a) own-source revenue may include more than tax receipts, and (b) this ratio does not include mean costs to individuals of other local fees and taxes (e.g., user fees paid to autonomous authorities).

Chapter 3

1 The degrees-of-freedom problem is not uncommon in budgeting studies that use time-series data. For example, Crecine's (1969) seminal work on simulation of the operating budget had three or four years worth of data for three cities (Detroit, Pittsburgh, and Cleveland). Larkey's (1979) excellent evaluation of the GRS program contained fourteen to twenty years worth of data for five medium- to large-sized cities. The number of observations in the present study ranges from ten to twenty-one years. Admittedly, a degrees-of-freedom problem may exist, but cost constraints make it unavoidable.

Chapter 5

1 In New Jersey, this rescission meant a drop from $180 million to $110 million in 1981. As a result, available federal money fell from $200 million per year (1972–1981 average) to $100 million per year (projected from 1982–1985) (*Conference on New Jersey's Infrastructure Bank* 1983).

2 As Pagano (1984, 3) notes:

Not until 1976 were Federal Aid highway funds allowed for activities other than construction. In the 1976 legislation construction was redefined as Resurfacing, Restoration and Rehabilitation (3R), making these activities eligible for federal highway funds. . . . The 1981 highway act, which followed a popular media blitz of the "deteriorating infrastructure" problem, expanded the term construction to include the fourth "R" or Reconstruction. . . . The wastewater construction grant program, on the other hand, has no comparable maintenance component. It has always been strictly a capital program. The 1981 changes disallow federal funding of wastewater treatment capacity expansion due to population growth—now, that is to be financed by the locality.

3 The 1978 report is considered to be the first report in spite of amendments to the 1970 Urban Growth and New Community Development Act that required a biennial presidential report. The 1972, 1974, and 1976 "reports" were severely criticized by local and state government officials, Congress, and urban public interest groups for not acknowledging that an urban crisis existed, let

alone proposing policies to address the crisis. Indeed, the Nixon and Ford administrations asserted that there was no urban crisis (see Stowe 1980).

4 More recent statements, such as those by the President's Commission for a National Agenda for the Eighties (1980) and the National Research Council (1982), are either non- or anti-urban in focus or explore issues that are well beyond the scope of an urban policy. This move away from a national focus on urban problems is even more explicit in the 1982 *National Urban Policy Report* (U.S. President 1982).

5 As Nathan, Doolittle, and Associates (1983) note, however, wastewater treatment grants had a 1981 budget authority of $3.3 billion prior to rescission of $1.7 billion. Thus, the increase to $2.4 billion is an increase only in terms of post-rescission authority. In terms of original 1981 budget authority, it is in fact a decrease.

6 The deteriorating quality of tax-exempt debt can be seen in several ways: the problem of servicing existing debt, the reliance of local governments on short-term debt, the introduction of many creative finance options, etc. These uncertain qualities of current state and local debt worry investors and rating agencies, which have responded by downgrading credit ratings. Petersen and Hough (1983, 18) note the response: during the first eight months of 1982, Moody's reduced the rating on almost twice as many tax exempts as they raised. "The 384 downgradings . . . were more than four times as many as were reported for all of 1979."

Bibliography

Abrams, Jay H. (1983). Financing Capital Expenditures: A Look at the Municipal Bond Market. *Public Administration Review* 43:378–82.

Advisory Commission on Intergovernmental Relations (1971). *Measuring the Fiscal Capacity of State and Effort of State and Local Areas.* Washington, D.C.: U.S. Government Printing Office.

Advisory Commission on Intergovernmental Relations (1977). *Federal Grants: Their Effects on State and Local Expenditures, Employment Levels, Wage Rates.* Washington, D.C.: U.S. Government Printing Office.

Advisory Commission on Intergovernmental Relations (1978). *Categorical Grants: Their Role and Design.* Washington, D.C.: U.S. Government Printing Office.

American Public Works Association (1979). *Administration of State Capital Improvement Program: Nine Selected Profiles.* Special Report No. 45. Chicago: American Public Works Association.

American Society of Planning Officials (1977). *Local Capital Improvements and Development Management.* Washington, D.C.: U.S. Department of Housing and Urban Development.

Aronson, J. Richard, and King, Arthur E. (1978). Is There a Fiscal Crisis Outside New York? *National Tax Journal* 31:153–64.

Aronson, J. Richard, and Schwartz, Eli (1975). Capital Budgeting. In *Management Policies in Local Government Finance*, ed. J. Richard Aronson and Eli Schwartz, pp. 303–32. Washington, D.C.: International City Management Association.

Auletta, Ken (1975). *The Streets Were Paved with Gold.* New York: Vintage.

Bahl, Roy, ed. (1981). *Urban Government Finance.* Beverly Hills: Sage.

Bahl, Roy (1982). The Administration's 1982 National Urban Policy Report. Prepared testimony. In *Hearings before the Joint Economic Committee, U.S. Congress.* Washington, D.C.: U.S. Government Printing Office.

Bahl, Roy (1984). *Financing State and Local Government in the 1980s.* New York: Oxford University Press.

Bahl, Roy; Jump, Bernard; and Schroeder, Larry (1978). The Outlook for City Fiscal Performance in Declining Regions. In *The Fiscal Outlook for Cities*, ed. Roy Bahl, pp. 1–48. Syracuse: Syracuse University Press.

Bahl, Roy, and Schroeder, Larry (1981). Fiscal Adjustments in Declining States. In *Cities Under Stress*, ed. Robert Burchell and David Listokin, pp. 301–32. New Brunswick: Rutgers University Press.

Barkin, Michael, and Wildavsky, Aaron, eds. (1982). *The Federal Government: Economics and Politics*. San Francisco: Institute for Contemporary Problems.

Barro, Stephen (1978). *The Urban Impacts of Federal Policies: Volume 3, Fiscal Conditions*. Santa Monica, Calif.: Rand Corporation.

Bearse, Peter J. ed. (1982). *Mobilizing Capital: Program Innovation and the Changing Public/Private Interface in Development Finance*. New York: Elsevier.

Bish, Robert L. (1971). *The Public Economy of Metropolitan Areas*. Chicago: Markham Publishing House.

Black, J. Thomas (1981). The Changing Economic Role of Central Cities and Suburbs. In *The Prospective City*, ed. Arthur P. Solomon, pp. 80–125. Cambridge: MIT Press.

Blair, John, and Nachmias, David, eds. (1979). *Fiscal Retrenchment and Urban Policy*. Beverly Hills: Sage Publications.

Board of Governors, Federal Reserve System (1982). *Flow of Funds Account*. December. Washington, D.C.: U.S. Federal Reserve System.

Bradbury, Katharine L. (1979). Concepts and Measures of City Fiscal Stress. Paper presented at the Eastern Economic Association Meeting, Boston, 10–12 May.

Bradbury, Katharine L., and Downs, Anthony, ed. (1981). *Do Housing Allowances Work?* Washington, D.C.: Brookings Institution.

Bradbury, Katharine L.; Downs, Anthony; and Small, Kenneth (1982). *Urban Decline and the Future of American Cities*. Washington, D.C.: Brookings Institution.

Browne, Lynn, and Syron, Richard (1977). Big City Bonds after New York. *New England Economic Review* (July): 11–26.

Broyd, Richard (1980). The Government Sector in Regional Models: A Comprehensive Treatment of the New York State Budget. *Discussion Papers in Environmental Health Planning*. Ithaca, N.Y.: Cornell University, Program in Urban and Regional Issues.

Burchell, Robert W., and Listokin, David (1981). *Cities Under Stress*. New Brunswick, N.J.: Rutgers University, Center for Policy Research.

Business Week (1981). Special Report: State and Local Government in Trouble. 26 October, 135–81.

Chinitz, Benjamin (1960). *Freight and the Metropolis*. Cambridge: Harvard University Press.

Choate, Pat (1980). *As Time Goes By: The Costs and Consequences of Delay*. Columbus, Ohio: Academy for Contemporary Problems.

Choate, Pat (1981). The Case for a National Capital Budget. *Public Budgeting and Finance* 1:21–26.

Choate, Pat, and Walter, Susan (1981). *America in Ruins: Beyond the Public Works Pork Barrel*. Washington, D.C.: Council of State Planning Agencies.

Clark, Terry N. (1981). Introduction: Community Development and Fiscal Strain. *Urban Affairs Papers* 3:1–12.

Clark, Terry Nichols, et al. (1976). *How Many New Yorks? The New York Fiscal Crisis in Comparative Perspective*. Comparative Study of Community Decision-Making, Research Report 72. Chicago: University of Chicago.

Clark, Terry N., and Ferguson, Lorna C. (1983). *City Money: Political Processes,*

Fiscal Strain, and Retrenchment. New York: Columbia University Press.

Clark, Terry Nichols, and Fuchs, Ester (1977). How We Measured Fiscal Strain. *Boston Globe* 11 January.

Clarke, Susan, and Rich, Michael (1982). Financial Federalism. Paper delivered at annual meeting of American Political Science Association, Denver, Colorado, September.

Cline, Robert J., and Shannon, John (1982). Municipal Revenue Behavior after Proposition 13. *Intergovernmental Perspectives* 8: 22–28.

Colman, William (1983). A Quiet Revolution in Local Government Finance. *Occasional Papers of the National Academy of Public Administration*, November.

Committee for Economic Development (1982). *Public-Private Partnership: An Opportunity for Urban Communities*. New York: Committee for Economic Development.

Conference on New Jersey's Infrastructure Bank Proposal (1983). Princeton: Woodrow Wilson School of Public and International Affairs, Princeton University.

Congressional Budget Office (1983). *Public Works Infrastructure: Policy Considerations for the 1980s*. Washington, D.C.: U.S. Government Printing Office.

Congressional Quarterly Weekly Report (1982). Politics, Price Tag Threatens Repair Program. 20 November, 2875–78.

CONSAD Research Corporation (1980). *A Study of Public Works Investment in the U.S.* 4 volumes. Prepared for the U.S. Department of Commerce. Pittsburgh: CONSAD Research Corporation.

Cornia, Gary, and Usher, Charles (1981). The Institutionalization of Incrementalism in Municipal Budgeting. *Southern Review of Public Administration* 5:73–90.

Crecine, John P. (1969). *Governmental Problem Solving*. Chicago: Rand McNally.

Crowley, Lyle, and Weisberg, Jacob (1982). The Road to Ruin. *Washington Monthly* September, 48–51.

Dames and Moore, Inc. (1978). *Analysis of Operations and Maintenance Costs for Municipal Wastewater Treatment Systems*. Washington, D.C.: U.S. Environmental Protection Agency.

Danziger, James (1976). *Making Budgets*. Beverly Hills: Sage.

Dean, Robert (1972–73). Plant Location Decision Processes. *Review of Regional Studies* 3:1–13.

DeVoy, R. S., and Wise, H., with Towles, J. (1979). *The Capital Budget*. Washington, D.C.: Council of State Planning Agencies.

Drucker, Peter (1973). Managing the Public Service Institution. *The Public Interest* 33:43–60.

Dye, Thomas, and Garcia, John A. (1978). Structure, Function, and Policy in American Cities. *Urban Affairs Quarterly* 14:103–22.

Ellwood, John (1982). *Reductions in U.S. Domestic Spending*. New Brunswick: Transaction Books.

Engineering News-Record (1978). Engineering News-Record Cost Indexes for 22 Cities. March.

Fainstein, Susan, and Fainstein, Norman (1976). The Federally Inspired Fiscal Crisis. *Society* 13:27–32.

Fleischmann, Arnold (1977). Sunbelt Boosterism: The Politics of Postwar Growth and Annexation in San Antonio. In *The Rise of Sunbelt Cities*, ed. David Perry and Alfred Watkins, pp. 151–68. Beverly Hills: Sage.

Forbes, Ronald, and Petersen, John (1976). *Building a Broader Market: Report of the Twentieth Century Fund Task Force on the Municipal Bond Market*. New York: McGraw-Hill.

Fosler, R. Scott, and Berger, Renee A., ed. (1982). *Public/Private Partnership in American Cities*. Lexington: Lexington Books.

Fossett, James W., and Nathan, Richard P. (1983). The Prospects for Urban Revival. In *Urban Government Finance: Emerging Trends*, ed. Roy Bahl, pp. 63–104. Beverly Hills: Sage.

Freiser, Joel (1982). The Urban Development Action Grant Program. In *Mobilizing Capital*, ed. Peter Bearse, chap. 13. New York: Elsevier.

Friedland, Roger (1981). Central City Fiscal Strain: The Public Costs of Private Growth. *International Journal of Urban and Regional Research* 5:356–75.

Friedmann, John (1966). *Regional Development Policy: A Case Study of Venezuela*. Cambridge: MIT Press.

Fuchs, Victor (1962). *Changes in the Location of Manufacturing in the United States since 1929*. New Haven: Yale University Press.

Gerard, Karen (1976). The Locally Inspired Fiscal Crisis. *Society* 13:33–35.

Glickman, Norman J., ed. (1980). *The Urban Impacts of Federal Policies*. Baltimore: Johns Hopkins University Press.

Goldmark, Peter (1982). The Federal Capital Investment Budget Act of 1982. Prepared testimony. In *Hearings before the Committee on Public Works and Transportation*, U.S. House. Washington, D.C.: U.S. Government Printing Office.

Golembiewski, Robert, and Rabin, Jack, eds. (1975). *Public Budgeting and Finance*. Itasca, Ill.: Peacock Publishers.

Goodman, Robert (1979). *The Last Entrepreneurs: America's Regional Wars for Jobs and Dollars*. New York: Simon and Schuster.

Goodrich, Carter (1960). *Government Promotion of Railroads and Canals*. New York: Columbia University Press.

Gramlich, Edward (1969). State and Local Goverments and Their Budget Constraints. *International Economic Review* 10:163–82.

Gramlich, Edward (1976). New York City Fiscal Crisis: What Happened and What Is To Be Done? *American Economic Review* 66:415–28.

Gramlich, Edward (1978). State and Local Budgets the Day after It Rained: Why Is the Surplus so High? *Brookings Papers on Economic Activity* 1:191–216.

Gramlich, Edward, and Galper, Harvey (1973). State and Local Fiscal Behavior and Federal Grant Policy. *Brookings Papers on Economic Activity* 1: 15–65.

Grossman, David (1977). *Capital Construction Needs of New York City in the 1977–1986 Period: A Preliminary Report*. New York: Twentieth Century Fund.

Haar, Charles M., et al. (1972). *Metropolitanization and Public Services*. Resources for the Future. Baltimore: Johns Hopkins Press.

Hamilton, Randy (1983). The World Turned Upside Down: The Contemporary Revolution in State and Local Government Capital Financing. *Public Administration Review* 43:22–31.

Hansen, Niles (1965). Municipal Investment Requirements in a Growing Agglomeration. *Land Economics* 41:49–56.

Hanson, Royce, ed. (1984). *Perspectives on Urban Infrastructure.* Washington, D.C.: National Academy Press.

Harrigan, John J. (1980). *Political Change in the Metropolis.* Boston: Little Brown.

Hartz, Louis (1968). *Economic Policy and Democratic Thought: Pennsylvania, 1776–1860.* Chicago: Quadrangle Books.

Hatry, Harry (1982). *Maintaining the Existing Infrastructure: Overview of Current Issues and Practices in Local Government Planning.* Washington, D.C.: U.S. Department of Housing and Urban Development.

Hayes, Frederick, et al. (1982). *Linkages: Improving Financial Management in Local Government.* Washington, D.C.: Urban Institute.

Helfand, Gary (1976). *Metropolitan Areas, Metropolitan Governments: A Reader.* Dubuque, Iowa: Kendall/Hunt Publishing Co.

Hicks, Donald (1982). Urban and Economic Adjustments to the Post-Industrial Era. Prepared testimony. In *Hearings before the Joint Economic Committee, U.S. Congress.* Washington, D.C.: U.S. Government Printing Office.

Hirschman, Albert O. (1958). *The Strategy of Economic Development.* New Haven: Yale University Press.

Hirschman, Albert O. (1967). *Development Projects Observed.* Washington, D.C.: Brookings Institution.

Holland, Stuart (1976). *Capital versus the Regions.* New York: St. Martin's.

Hoover, Edgar (1948). *The Location of Economic Activity.* New York: McGraw-Hill.

Horowitz, A. L. (1968). A Simultaneous Equation Approach to the Problem of Explaining Interstate Differences in State and Local Government Expenditures. *Southern Economic Journal* 34:559–76.

Hoskins, Ronald (1984). Selected Determinants of Appropriations Changes during Budget Execution in Georgia State Government. Paper presented at the annual meeting of the American Political Science Association, Washington, D.C., September.

Howard, S. Kenneth (1973). *Changing State Budgeting.* Lexington, Ky.: Council of State Governments.

Huckins, Larry and Tolley, George (1981). Investments in Local Infrastructure. In *Urban Policy Analysis,* ed. Terry Clark, pp. 123–32. Beverly Hills: Sage.

Humphrey, Nancy, et al. (1980). *Restructuring of Baltimore's Water and Wastewater Utilities—Organizational and Financial Considerations.* Washington, D.C.: Urban Institute.

Inman, Robert (1979). Fiscal Performance of Local Governments. In *Current Issues in Urban Economics,* ed. Peter Mieszkowski and Mahlon Straszheim, pp. 270–321. Baltimore: Johns Hopkins University Press.

Isard, Walter (1956). *Location and Space-Economy.* Cambridge: MIT Press.

Johnson, S. R., and Junk, P. E. (1970). Sources of Tax Revenues and Expenditures in Large U.S. Cities. *Quarterly Review of Economics and Business* 10:7–15.

Judd, Dennis, and Collins, Margaret (1979). The Case of Tourism: Political Coalitions and Redevelopment in the Central Cities. In *The Changing Structure of the Cities*. ed. Gary Tobin, pp. 177–200. Beverly Hills: Sage.

Kain, John (1978). Failure in Diagnosis: A Critique of Carter's National Urban Policy. *Policy Note* P78-2. Cambridge: Harvard University, Department of City and Regional Planning.

Key, V. O., Jr. (1940). The Lack of a Budgetary Theory. *American Political Science Review* 34:1137–44.

Kidwell, David S., and Rogowski, Robert J. (1983). Bond Banks: A State Assistance Program that Helps Reduce New Issue Borrowing Costs. *Public Administration Review* 43:108–13.

King, Timothy, and Barkin, David (1970). *Regional Economic Development: The River Basin Approach in Mexico*. Cambridge: Cambridge University Press.

Lake, Robert (1983). New Jersey's Infrastructure Needs: A Case Study. Mimeographed. New Brunswick: Center For Urban Policy Research, Rutgers University.

Lampard, Eric (1968). The Evolving System of Cities in the United States: Urbanization and Economic Development. In *Issues in Urban Economics*, ed. Harvey Perloff and Lowdon Wingo, Jr., pp. 81–139. Resources for the Future. Baltimore: Johns Hopkins University Press.

Larkey, Patrick (1979). *Evaluating Public Programs*. Princeton: Princeton University Press.

Lehman Brothers Kuhn Loeb (1984). *Public Infrastructure: Problems, Priorities, and Financing Alternatives*. New York: Lehman Brothers Kuhn Loeb.

Levine, Charles H. (1978). Organizational Decline and Cutback Management. *Public Administration Review* 38:316–25.

Levine, Charles H. (1980). Management Constraints in the Face of Budget Constraints. In *Managing Fiscal Retrenchment in Cities*, ed. Harrington Bryce, chap. 3. National Urban Policy Roundtable. Columbus, Ohio: Academy for Contemporary Problems.

Levine, Charles H., and Rubin, Irene, eds. (1980). *Fiscal Stress and Public Policy*. Beverly Hills: Sage.

Levine, Charles H.; Rubin, Irene; and Wolohojian, George (1981). *The Politics of Retrenchment*. Beverly Hills: Sage

Liebert, Roland (1979). *Disintegration and Political Action*. New York: Academic Press.

Lindblom, Charles, and Braybrooke, David (1963). *A Strategy of Decision: Policy Evaluation as a Social Process*. New York: Free Press of Glencoe.

Lineberry, Robert, and Masotti, Louis (1976). Introduction. In *The New Urban Politics*, ed. L. Masotti and R. Lineberry, pp. 1–35. Cambridge: Ballinger Publishing Company.

Litvak, Lawrence, and Daniels, Belden (1979). *Innovations in Development Finance*. Washington, D.C.: Council of State Planning Agencies.

Losch, August (1954). *The Economics of Location*. New Haven: Yale University Press.

Lovell, Catherine (1981). Evolving Local Government Dependency. *Public Administration Review* 41:189–202.

Lovell, Catherine, and Tobin, Charles (1981). The Mandate Issue. *Public Administration Review* 41:318–31.

Lowi, Theodore (1964). American Business, Public Policy, Case Studies, and

Political Theory. *World Politics* 16:677–715.

McCracken, Paul (1977). The Economy and the Federal Budget. Prepared testimony. *Hearings before the Committee on the Budget,* U.S. Senate. Washington, D.C.: U.S. Government Printing Office.

McGouldrick, Paul F., and Petersen, John (1968). Monetary Restraint and Borrowing and Capital Spending by Large State and Local Governments in 1966. *Federal Reserve Bulletin* 54:552–81.

McGowan, Robert P., and Stevens, John M. (1983). Local Government Initiatives in a Climate of Uncertainty. *Public Administration Review* 43:127–36.

MacManus, Susan (1978). *Revenue Patterns in U.S. Cities and Suburbs: A Comparative Analysis.* New York: Praeger.

McMillan, T. E., Jr. (1965). Why Manufacturers Choose Plant Locations versus Determinants of Plant Locations. *Land Economics* 41:239–46.

Manvel, Allen D. (1963). Changing Patterns of Local Urban Expenditures. In *Public Expenditure Decisions in the Urban Community*, ed. A. Schaller, pp. 19–36. Washington, D.C.: Resources for the Future.

Manvel, Allen D. (1965). State and Local Government Financing of Capital Outlays, 1946–1965. In *State and Local Public Facility Needs and Financing*, U.S. Congress, Joint Economic Committee, vol. 2. Washington, D.C.: U.S. Government Printing Office.

Matz, Deborah (1981). The Tax and Expenditure Limitation Movement. In *Urban Government Finance: Emerging Trends*, ed. Roy Bahl, pp. 127–54. Beverly Hills: Sage.

Matz, Deborah, and Petersen, John (1982). *Trends in the Fiscal Conditions of Cities, 1980–1982.* U.S. Congress, Joint Economic Committee. Washington, D.C.: U.S. Government Printing Office.

Meltsner, Arnold (1971). *The Politics of City Revenue.* Berkeley: University of California Press.

Metropolitan Sewer District (1967–77). *Annual Reports.* Hartford, Conn.: Metropolitan Sewer District.

Metropolitan St. Louis Sewer District (1958–77). *Audited Financial Accounts.* St. Louis, Mo.: Metropolitan St. Louis Sewer District.

Meyer, John, and Quigley, John (1977). *Local Public Finance and the Fiscal Squeeze: A Case Study.* Cambridge, Mass.: Ballinger.

Miernyk, William (1976). Decline of the Northern Perimeter. *Society* 13:24–26.

Mikesell, John (1982). *Fiscal Administration.* Homewood, Ill.: Dorsey Press.

Miller, Gary (1982). *Cities by Contract.* Cambridge: MIT Press.

Mollenkopf, John (1983). *The Contested City.* Princeton: Princeton University Press.

Moore, Richard J., and Beer, Nancy (1984). *Lessons in New Jersey's Infrastructure Bank Proposal.* Princeton Urban and Regional Research Center, Working Paper No. 5. Princeton: Princeton University.

Moore, Richard J., and Pagano, Michael A. (1982a). Emerging Issues in Financing Basic Infrastructure. In *Mobilizing Capital: Program Innovation and the Changing Public/Private Interface in Development Finance*, ed. Peter Bearse, pp. 423–48. New York: Elsevier.

Moore, Richard J., and Pagano, Michael A. (1982b). Aid for Urban Infrastructure:

The Bias against Declining Cities. *Economic Development Commentary* 6:14-18.

Moore, Richard J., and Pagano, Michael A. (1983). Capital Formation, Supply-Side Economics, and the Public Sector. *Southern Review of Public Administration* 6:450-64.

Morgan Guaranty Trust (1982). Rebuilding America's Infrastructure. *The Morgan Guaranty Survey* (July): 11-18.

Mountjoy, Alan B. (1966). *Industrialization and Underdeveloped Countries.* London: Hutchinson and Company.

Moynihan, Daniel P. (1979). New York City and the Federal Fisc, III: Fiscal Year 1978. Statement by Senator Moynihan, 10 June.

Muller, Thomas (1975). *Growing and Declining Urban Areas: A Fiscal Comparison.* Washington, D.C.: Urban Institute.

Municipal Finance Officers Association, Government Finance Research Center (1984). *Building Prosperity: Financing Public Infrastructure for Economic Development.* Washington, D.C.: Municipal Finance Officers Association.

Musgrave, Richard A. (1959). *The Theory of Public Finance.* New York: McGraw-Hill.

Mushkin, Selma (1979). The Case for User Fees. *Taxes and Spending* (April): 49-62.

Mushkin, Selma, and Vehorn, Charles L. (1977). User Fees and Charges. *Government Finance* 6:61-75.

Myrdal, Gunnar (1957). *Economic Theory and the Underdeveloped Regions.* London: G. Duckworth and Company.

Nathan, Richard, and Adams, Charles (1976). Understanding Central City Hardship. *Political Science Quarterly* 92:47-62.

Nathan, Richard; Adams, Charles; and Associates (1977). *Revenue Sharing: The Second Round.* Washington, D.C.: Brookings Institution.

Nathan, Richard, and Dommel, Paul (1978). Federal Local Relations Under Block Grants. *Political Science Quarterly* 83:421-42.

Nathan, Richard; Doolittle, Fred; and Associates (1983). *The Consequences of Cuts: The Effects of the Reagan Domestic Program on State and Local Government.* Princeton: Princeton Urban and Regional Research Center.

Nathan, Richard, and Fossett, James W. (1979). Urban Conditions: The Future of the Federal Role. *Proceedings of the 71st Annual Convention of the National Tax Association/Tax Institute of America.* Columbus, Ohio: National Tax Association.

Nathan, Richard; Manvel, Allen; Calkins, Susannah; and Associates (1975). *Monitoring Revenue Sharing.* Washington, D.C.: Brookings Institution.

Nathan, Richard, et al. (1977). Monitoring the Block Grant Program for Community Development. *Political Science Quarterly* 92:219-44.

Nathan, Richard, et al. (1979). *Monitoring the Public Service Employment Program: The Second Round.* Washington: National Commission on Manpower Policy.

Nathan, Richard, et al. (1981). *Public Service Employment: A Field Evaluation.* Washington, D.C.: Brookings Institution.

National Infrastructure Advisory Committee (1984). *Hard Choices: A Report on the Increasing Gap between America's Infrastructure Needs and Our Ability to Pay for Them*. Prepared for the U.S. Congress, Joint Economic Committee. Washington, D.C.: U.S. Government Printing Office.

National Journal (1983). Capital May Not Be the Key to Productivity. 16 April, p. 820.

National League of Cities/U.S. Conference of Mayors (1983). *Capital Budgeting and Infrastructure in American Cities: An Initial Assessment*. Washington, D.C.: National League of Cities.

National Research Council (1980). *The New CETA: Effects on Public Service Employment Programs: Final Report*. Washington, D.C.: National Academy Press.

National Research Council (1981). *Critical Issues for National Urban Policy: A Reconnaissance and Agenda for Further Study*. Washington, D.C.: National Academy Press.

Netzer, Dick (1968). Federal, State, and Local Finance in a Metropolitan Context. In *Issues in Urban Economics*, ed. Harvey Perloff and Lowdon Wingo, pp. 435–76. Baltimore: John Hopkins University Press.

Neutze, G. M. (1967). Major Determinants of Location Patterns. *Land Economics* 43:227–32.

New Jersey Municipalities (1983). New Jersey's Crumbling Infrastructure. April, pp. 6–26.

New Orleans, City of (1978). *Mayor's Capital Budget Recommendations for Five-Year Capital Program, 1979–1983*. New Orleans: Office of the Mayor.

Newsweek (1982). The Decaying of America: Our Dams, Bridges, Roads, and Water Systems Are Rapidly Falling Apart. 2 August, pp. 12–20.

Noah, Timothy (1982). Bring Back the WPA. *Washington Monthly* (September): 38–46.

North, Douglas (1955). Location Theory and Regional Economic Growth. *Journal of Political Economy* 53:243–58.

Norton, Robert D. (1979). *City-Life Cycles and American Urban Policy*. New York: Academic Press.

O'Connor, James (1973). *The Fiscal Crisis of the State*. New York: St. Martin's.

O'Day, D. Kelly, and Neumann, Lance (1983). Assessing Infrastructure Need: The State of the Art. Prepared for National Academy of Sciences, National Research Council Symposium on the Adequacy and Maintenance of Urban Public Facilities, Warrenton, Virginia, February.

Ohls, J. C. and Wales, T. J. (1972). Supply and Demand for State and Local Services. *Review of Economics and Statistics* 54:424–30.

Ott, David J., et al. (1975). *State-Local Finances in the Last Half of the 1970s*. Washington, D.C.: American Enterprise Institute.

Pagano, Michael A. (1980). Fiscal Stress and the Financing of Urban Infrastructure. Ph.D. dissertation, University of Texas at Austin.

Pagano, Michael A. (1982). The Urban Public Sector as Lagging or Leading Sector in Economic Development. *The Urban Interest* 4:131–40.

Pagano, Michael A. (1984). The New Federalism's Proposals for Infrastructure. Mimeographed. Oxford, Ohio: Miami University.

Pagano, Michael A. (forthcoming). Old Wine in New Bottles? An Analysis and

Preliminary Appraisal of the Surface Transportation Assistance Act of 1982. *Publius.*

Parade (1979). Our Bridges Are Falling Down. 7 January.

Pascal, Anthony (1980). *User Fees, Contracting Out, and Privatization in an Era of Fiscal Retrenchment.* Santa Monica: Rand Corporation.

Perry, David, and Watkins, Alfred, eds. (1977). *The Rise of Sunbelt Cities.* Beverly Hills: Sage.

Petersen, John E. (1976). *Changing Conditions in the Market for State and Local Debt.* Washington, D.C.: U.S. Government Printing Office.

Petersen, John E., and Wesley C. Hough (1983). *Creative Capital Financing.* Chicago: Municipal Finance Officers Association.

Peterson, George (1976). Finance. In *The Urban Predicament*, ed. William Gorham and Nathan Glazer, pp. 35–118. Washington, D.C.: The Urban Institute.

Peterson, George (1978). Capital Spending and Capital Obsolescence: The Outlook for Cities. In *The Fiscal Outlook for Cities*, ed. Roy Bahl, pp. 49–74. Syracuse: Syracuse University Press.

Peterson, George, ed. (1980–82). *The Future of America's Capital Plant.* 6 vols. Washington, D.C.: Urban Institute.

Peterson, George (1981). Transmitting the Municipal Fiscal Squeeze to a New Generation of Taxpayers: Pension Obligations and Capital Investments. In *Cities Under Stress: The Fiscal Crisis of Urban America*, ed. Robert Burchell and David Listokin, pp. 249–76. New Brunswick, N.J.: Center for Urban Policy Research.

Peterson, George E. (1984). Financing the Nation's Infrastructure Requirements. In *Perspectives on Urban Infrastructure*, ed. Royce Hanson, pp. 110–42. Washington, D.C.: National Academy Press.

Peterson, Paul (1981). *City Limits.* Chicago: University of Chicago Press.

Pittsburgh Post-Gazette (1979). County Sanitary Sewers Failing: Repairs May Soar to $1/2 Billion. 18 April.

Port Authority of New York and New Jersey (1984). *Proposal for a National Infrastructure Bank.* New York: Port Authority.

President's Commission for a National Agenda for the Eighties (1980). *Urban America in the 1980s.* Washington, D.C.: U.S. Government Printing Office.

Reagan, Michael D. and Sanzone, John (1981). *The New Federalism.* New York: Oxford University Press.

Regional Plan Association (1982). Economic Development and Public Infrastructure Investment for the New York Urban Region. Prepared for the U.S. Department of Commerce. Mimeographed.

Reischauer, Robert D. (1978). The Economy, The Federal Budget, and the Prospects for Urban Aid. In *The Fiscal Outlook for Cities: Implications of a National Urban Policy*, ed. Roy Bahl, pp. 93–110. Syracuse: Syracuse University Press.

Reischauer, Robert D. (1981). The Economy and the Federal Budget in the 1980s: Implications for the State and Local Sector. In *Urban Government Finance: Emerging Trends*, ed. Roy Bahl, pp. 13–38. Beverly Hills: Sage.

Richardson, Harry (1969). *Regional Economics.* New York: Praeger Publications.

Richardson, Harry (1979). The State of Regional Economics: A Survey Article.

International Regional Science Review 3:1–48.

Rittenoure, R. Lynn, and Pluta, Joseph (1977). Theory of Intergovernmental Grants and Local Government. *Growth and Change* (July): 31–37.

Rosenthal, Donald, ed. (1980). *Urban Revitalization*. Beverly Hills: Sage.

Sanders, Heywood T. (1984). Politics and Urban Public Facilities. In *Perspectives on Urban Infrastructure*. ed. Royce Hanson, pp. 143–77. Washington, D.C.: National Academy Press.

Savas, E. S. (1981). *Privatizing the Public Sector*. Chatham, N.J.: Chatham House Publishers.

Sawers, Larry, and Tabb, William K., eds. (1984). *Sunbelt, Snowbelt: Urban Development and Regional Restructuring*. New York: Oxford University Press.

Schatz, Sayre (1972). The Role of Capital Accumulation in Economic Development. In *Readings in Economic Development*, ed. Walter Johnson and David Kamerschen, pp. 345–49. Cincinnati: Southwestern Publishing Company.

Schill, Michael, and Nathan, Richard (1983). *Revitalizing America's Cities*. Albany: SUNY Press.

Schneiderman, Paul (1975). State and Local Government Fixed Capital Formation, 1958–1973. *Survey of Current Business* (October): 17–25.

Schultze, Charles, et al. (1976). Fiscal Problems of Cities. In *The Fiscal Crisis of American Cities*, ed. Roger Alcaly and David Mermelstein, pp. 189–212. New York: Vantage.

Seattle, City of (1977). *Official Bond Offering Statement*. Seattle: City of Seattle.

Sinding, Rick (1983). The Infrastructure Bank: Assets and Liabilities. *New Jersey Reporter* (February): 6–12.

Smith, David (1968). The Response of State and Local Governments to Federal Grants. *National Tax Journal* 21:349–57.

Stein, Robert (1982). The Structural Character of Federal Aid: An Examination of Fiscal Impact. Paper delivered at the 1982 annual meeting of the American Political Science Association, Denver, Colorado, September.

Steiss, Alan Walter (1975). *Local Government Finance*. Lexington, Mass.: Lexington Books.

Stowe, Eric L. (1980). Defining a National Urban Policy. In *Urban Revitalization*, ed. D. Rosenthal, pp. 145–64. Beverly Hills: Sage.

Tabb, William, and Sawers, Larry, eds. (1978). *Marxism and the Metropolis*. New York: Oxford University Press.

Thompson, Wilbur (1965). *A Preface to Urban Economics*. Washington, D.C.: Resources for the Future.

Tiebout, Charles (1956). A Pure Theory of Public Expenditures. *Journal of Political Economy* 44:416–24.

Tobin, Gary, ed. (1979). *The Changing Structure of the City*. Beverly Hills: Sage.

Tobin, Gary (1983). The Public/Private Sector Partnership in the Redevelopment Process. *Policy Studies Journal* 11:473–82.

Tobin, James (1982). The Wrong Mix for Recovery. *Challenge* (May/June): 21–27.

Touche Ross and Company (1979). *Urban Fiscal Stress: A Comparative Analysis of 66 Cities*. Boston: First National Bank of Boston and Touche Ross and Company.

U.S. Bureau of Labor Statistics (1957–77). *Union Wages and Hours: Building Trades*. Washington, D.C.: U.S. Government Printing Office.

U.S. Conference of Mayors (1982). *The FY82 Budget and the Cities*. Washington, D.C.: U.S. Conference of Mayors.

U.S. Congress, Joint Economic Committee (1979). *Deteriorating Infrastructure in Urban and Rural Areas*. Washington, D.C.: U.S. Government Printing Office.

U.S. Congress, Senate Committee on Environment and Public Works (1983). *Infrastructure and Jobs*. Washington, D.C.: U.S. Government Printing Office.

U.S. Department of Commerce (1975). *Annual Survey of Manufacturing*. Washington, D.C.: U.S. Government Printing Office.

U.S. Department of Commerce, Bureau of the Census, (1960–75). *County and City Data Book*. Washington, D.C.: U.S. Government Printing Office.

U.S. Department of Commerce, Bureau of the Census (1957–83). *City Government Finances*. Washington, D.C.: U.S. Government Printing Office.

U.S. Department of Commerce, Bureau of the Census (1957–77). *Finances of Special Districts*. Washington, D.C.: U.S. Government Printing Office.

U.S. Department of Commerce, Bureau of the Census (1957–83). *Government Finances*. Washington, D.C.: U.S. Government Printing Office.

U.S. Department of Transportation, Federal Highway Administration (1975). *National Highway Inventory and Performance Study Manual*. Washington: U.S. Department of Transportation.

U.S. Department of Treasury, Office of State and Local Finances (1978). *Report on the Fiscal Impact of the Economic Stimulus Package on 48 Large Urban Governments*. Washington, D.C.: U.S. Department of the Treasury.

U.S. Environmental Protection Agency (1977). *U.S. Environmental Protection Agency Sewer and Sewage Treatment Plant Index*. Washington, D.C.: U.S. EPA.

U.S. Environmental Protection Agency (1982). *The 1982 Needs Survey*. Washington: U.S. EPA.

U.S. General Accounting Office (1982). *Effective Planning and Budgeting Practices Can Help Arrest the Nation's Deteriorating Public Infrastructure*. Washington, D.C.: U.S. Government Printing Office.

U.S. General Accounting Office (1981). *Federal Capital Budgeting: A Collection of Haphazard Practices*. Washington, D.C.: U.S. Government Printing Office.

U.S. News and World Report (1982). To Rebuild America: $2,500,000,000,000 Job. 27 September, pp. 8–19.

U.S. President (1978, 1980, 1982). *National Urban Policy Report*. Prepared by the Department of Housing and Urban Development. Washington, D.C.: U.S. Government Printing Office.

U.S. President, Office of Management and Budget (1957–84). *Special Analyses, Budget of the United States*. Washington, D.C.: U.S. Government Printing Office.

Urban Land Institute (1983). Financing State and Local Infrastructure in a Time of Fiscal Constraint. *Urban Land* 3:4–24.

Vaughan, Roger (1977). *The Urban Impacts of Federal Policies: Volume 2, Economic Development*. Santa Monica: Rand Corporation.

Vaughan, Roger (1984). Rebuilding America: Financing Public Works in the 1980s. In *Rebuilding America's Infrastructure*, ed. Michael Barker, pp. 99–317. Durham: Duke University Press.

Wacht, Richard (1980). *A New Approach to Capital Budgeting for City and County Governments*. Research Monograph No. 87. Atlanta: College of Business Administration, Georgia State University.

Wasylenko, Michael (1981). The Location of Firms: The Role of Taxes and Fiscal Incentives. In *Urban Government Finance: Emerging Trends*, ed. Roy Bahl, pp. 155–90. Beverly Hills: Sage.

Waterston, Albert (1966). *Development Planning*. Syracuse: Syracuse University Press.

Webman, Jerry A. (1981). UDAG: Targeting Urban Economic Development. *Political Science Quarterly* 10:189–207.

Weinstein, Bernard L., and Clark, Robert J. (1981). The Fiscal Outlook for Growing Cities. In *Urban Government Finance: Emerging Trends*, ed. Roy Bahl, pp. 105–26. Beverly Hills: Sage.

White, Michael J. (1980). Capital Budgeting. In *Essays in Public Finance and Financial Management: State and Local Perspectives*, ed. John Petersen and Catherine L. Spain, pp. 42–52. Chatham, N.J.: Chatham House Publishers.

Whitman, Ray (1979). Effects of Federal Capital Grants on Five State-Local Functions: Sewage, Water Supply, Highways, Bridges and Mass Transit. Preliminary Draft. Washington, D.C.: Urban Institute.

Wiggins, C. Don (1980). A Case Study in Governmental Capital Budgeting. *Governmental Finance* 9:19–22.

Wildavsky, Aaron (1964). *The Politics of the Budgetary Process*. Boston: Little, Brown.

Wilde, James A. (1968). The Expenditure Effects of Grants-in-Aid Programs. *National Tax Journal* 21:340–47.

Wilde, James A. (1971). Grants-in-Aid: The Analytics of Design and Response. *National Tax Journal* 24:143–55.

Wolf, Charles (1979). A Theory of Non-Market Failures. *Public Interest* 55:114–33.

Wonnacott, Ronald, and Wonnacott, Thomas (1979). *Econometrics*. 2d ed. New York: John Wiley and Sons.

Yin, Robert (1979). Creeping Federalism: The Federal Impact on the Structure and Function of Local Government. Paper presented at the Conference on the Urban Impacts of Federal Policies, Johns Hopkins University, November.

Youngson, A. J. (1967). *Overhead Capital: A Study of the Development Economics*. Edinburgh: Edinburgh University Press.

Index